The Inner Circle Chronicles

Intuitive Visionary Women Leaders of the New Economy Transforming Lives and Businesses With Soul and Spirit

Book 5

Other books from Inner Visions Publishing:

Inner Circles Chronicles–Book 1
12 Intuitive Women Leaders of the New Economy, Transforming Lives and Businesses with Soul and Spirit

Inner Circles Chronicles–Book 2
Intuitive Women Leaders of the New Economy, Transforming Lives and Businesses with Divine Heart and Soul Around the World

Inner Circles Chronicles–Book 3
Intuitive Healers Leading the New Economy with Integrative Health, Soul, and Spirit

Inner Circles Chronicles–Book 4
Intuitive Leaders of the New Economy, Transforming Lives and Businesses with Global Consciousness and Spiritual Teachings

Books by Anne Deidre:

Extreme Intuitive Makeover–
55 Keys to Health, Wealth and Happiness

Miraculous–
How Spiritual Awakening Cured My Depression, Inspired My Purpose, and Ignited the Intuitive Powers Within

Intuition–
7 Basic Instincts to Change Your Life

The Inner Circle Chronicles

Intuitive Visionary Women Leaders of the New Economy Transforming Lives and Businesses With Soul and Spirit

Book 5

Inspired and Edited by
Anne Deidre

Anne Deidre
Inner Visions Publishing
Giving Voice to Spiritual, Intuitive Artists and Writers

New Hampshire

Published by Inner Visions Publishing

InnerVisionsPublishing.com

Edited by Anne Deidre
Cover Design & Layout Molly Sullivan

ISBN: 978-0-692-07643-9

Printed in the United States of America

This book is dedicated to all humankind.
May you recognize the Light within
and the ability to expand consciousness
on the planet through your very existence.
Peace within, Peace without.

The Inner Circle Chronicles

Intuitive Visionary Women Leaders of the New Economy Transforming Lives and Businesses With Soul and Spirit

Book 5

Table of Contents

The Starfish

Starfish are known to be able to regenerate an amputated limb. I chose the starfish for the cover of this book as I feel that the energy of regeneration and self healing is powerful and one that is shared by the women authors in this book.

We have a divine blueprint, divine potential, and it's an honor to share the stories of empowerment!

—book 5 of *The Inner Circle Chronicles.*

The Star Thrower

One day, an old man was walking along a beach that was littered with thousands of starfish that had been washed ashore by the high tide. As he walked, he came upon a young boy who was eagerly throwing the starfish back into the ocean, one by one.

Puzzled, the man looked at the boy and asked what he was doing. Without looking up from his task, the boy simply replied,
"I'm saving these starfish, Sir."

The old man chuckled aloud, "Son, there are thousands of starfish and only one of you. What difference can you make?"

The boy picked up a starfish, gently tossed it into the water and turning to the man, said, "I made a difference to that one!"

—Loren Eisley

Introduction

Within each of us holds our highest Divine potential. It is our great work to uncover that, excavate it, as our purpose is often buried beneath regret, remorse and fear of failure or success. We are enough. Expressing our uniqueness is what we came here to do. It can unfold throughout our lifetime, but to never begin, and stay stuck in any area of our lives and feeling miserable is not the journey we are here to take. Those failures, those feelings of unworthiness are here to be integrated in our experience so that the fullness of who we are as both human and Divine can be celebrated and transmuted into joy.

I have learned to value every experience. Transcending is an energy of mastery and working with the women of The Inner Circle Chronicles Book 5 has been inspiring and illuminating. Each one has a profound message of encouragement and possibility to go beyond what you ever thought was possible, where there is a will there is a way. An avatar I have worked with calls this Will Persistence. I call this Aligning my Will with Divine Will. The women of Book 5, took command of their energy, and with perseverance and great love, exemplify a true pioneering and trailblazing spirit.

The women in Book 5 are true Visionaries as they have all not just blindly accepted what anyone told them or were shown from our society about what is possible to achieve or attain in life. Attainment is a potent word, a spiritual word in that once you have attained a state of consciousness, it becomes a permanent state of your being. These women have attained a level of consciousness that told them they could do anything, and so they have. They have created their own standard, created and designed their own lives in their way, to serve their highest and greatest good and their works serve the greatest good of all. I can't think of a higher purpose and calling. It is an honor to share their stories.

May you be blessed as you read each one.

Anne Deidre

Anne Deidre is an International Celebrity Expert on Intuition, Certified Medical Intuitive, Best selling author and publisher, professional artist, speaker and coach. She has been featured on *ABC* and *NBC TV*, on *The CW TV Network, Huff Post Live*, also a *FOX News Radio* Contributor, on *NPR, CBS radio, Business Talk Radio,* and many print publications such as *Examiner.com*, *Belief* and *Aspire* magazine. Anne's work is channeled form the Divine Energy and Frequency that includes Spirit, Ascended Masters, Archangels, and each soul's Divine Self to shift energetic patterns, catalyze dormant gifts and talents, and ignite the Divine intuitive powers within each person.

Anne's transformational gifts allow her to intuitively shine a light into her clients' energy systems and illuminate their hidden and/or dormant Divine gifts to shift energetic patterns, heal trauma, and create new patterns so that they can bring their Divine gifts to the world.

Anne has created *Visionary Intuitive Academy* with platinum private and group coaching for future thought leaders. Spiritual teachers, and professional intuitives.

Anne Deidre
Bestselling Author, Speaker, Coach
Featured on HuffPost Live, NH Chronicle, ABC, NBC, CBS TV and a FOX News Radio Contributor

annedeidre.com
email: team@annedeidre.com

Diane Arnal

Diane Arnal is a certified angel card reader through Anne Deidre. Diane belongs to astrology group. Diane has joined a couple of light minded groups which is huge since she lives in St. George,Utah, she belong to a loving Red Tent group. She golfs every week.

What she really enjoys is sitting back and watching people and if she sees somebody that needs help. She likes to be able to help them. It may be by giving them a helping hand. She believes that we are all gods children and that we should love and respect each other with kindness and love nothing more nothing less just love love love.

—Love & Light

Diane_Arnal@msn.com

Before I began my story I would like to say how thankful I am to have Anne Deidre by my side. To have faith in me and giving me the opportunity to share my story.

Anne is such a sweetheart, she taught me how to read angel cards and to become certified, she is such a loving angel. I am so happy to see her grow into a beautiful flower. Her light is so bright that you almost need to wear sunglasses

My Story

(Everyone Has A Story —This Is Mine)

Diane Arnal

My name is Diane Arnal I am 71 years old. I am going to tell you a little bit about my background before I get started telling you where I am in my life today.

I was raised in Salt Lake City, Utah. I have been married four times. And I have no children, not by choice. The first time I was married I was 15 years old, married for 9 years. My husband at the time got involved with a group of polygamists. And still to this day he still would like to live per their teachings.

My second marriage was to a supervisor of mine at work. We were married for six weeks. Went to court and had the marriage annulled, because my husband had a live in girlfriend who said they were married. They were not legally married. But I told the lady that she could have him.

My third marriage was to a man that worked at a grocery store and supposedly he was assistant manager at the time. He was married when we got involved. This fellow also had two small boys. He then got a divorce and we lived together about two years. Then we got married. I helped him with the support of his wife and his two sons. This man that I married had a problem with alcohol and he had a wandering eye. When he came home from work he would be drunk. Then we would start to fight, first it was verbal then it would be physical. I don't know how many black eyes that I had. He broke my nose once and also popped my eardrum. I made that mistake of letting my mother see me with a black eye. So when I would have a black eye I would stay away from my mother. God lover her.

This went on for a period of time. We had a house built and things seem to settle down. We were in our home for six months. The fighting picked up again. So that marriage came to an end.

My fourth husband Paul John know as PJ died on my 60th birthday. I tell people that's when I started my spiritual journey.

I started picking up the pieces to the puzzle of my life, and that is where I also started to go within myself and ask who are you Diane?

I'm going to tell you a little more of my back ground. My whole way of thinking has changed 180°. Before my husband died I really didn't know who I was, what I liked and I didn't even pick up a book to read. I had worked all of my adult life until I was very fortunate enough to take a early retirement at the age of 56.

I had worked for a company for 34 1/2 years, and my late husband had worked at the same company for 28 years. My husband and I worked long hours, it was nothing for us to work 60 hours a week. We worked a lot of overtime at work, our days would start at 5 in the morning, so I was up every morning at 3:30am. I would come home, fix dinner, clean the mess, have a few drinks and watch television and go to bed, this would go on day in and day out. We didn't do much through the 30 years that we were a couple. My husband had his toys like his Pathfinder, a doom buggy to play in the sand. And his pride and joy his Harley Davidson. Oh yes our motor home.

I started picking up books and reading them, I would read one by one, authors like Sylvia Browne, I have all of her books. Then I got to Doreen Virtue and then I would read books by Gregg Braden. Then I started going to conferences in Las Vegas which had a list of speakers and classes that you could take and I really got involved and I really enjoyed them. I found a book to read and then I got another book to read. I got to the point where I realize I would have to read one book 1st before I went to the next to read in order to understand what I was reading.

Then I started playing golf and I met this fellow named Richard Mello and we started going out then we became a couple but we never married. As time went on we started living together and it was a wonderful relationship. He did his thing and I done mine. If I wanted to go to lunch with the girls or if I wanted to go to a conference out of town, I did. I did not have to ask and the same was with him. It was just one of those beautiful relationships that I had never experienced and I don't believe that he had either. I'll talk more about Richard at the end of my story.

Now I'm going to give you some more of my background about when I was a little girl and explain some of my experiences and my struggles that I had and I have some of these struggles to this day.

I have never told anybody about the struggles that I had. I am going to be sharing these with you. The only one that knew about my struggles was my late husband Paul John. And he was so loving and caring and very supportive.

And thank you Paul John I know you prefer going by PJ love and light. You will always be a part of my heart.

When I was a little girl, my precious mother was single and raising her three children by herself. She was on welfare for a short time. Then she was able to get herself a full-time job working at Toole depot. So my mother was gone.

I remember when I started school I really struggled. When I talked I stuttered. So they put me in a speech class. Then when it came to reading I had a hard time sounding out the words. This went on for me for many years. I was able to get through school but it was real struggle. I remember being in fourth or fifth grade and I was still struggling sounding out my words. I had a teacher that would put her slow students in the back of the class give us a copy of Reader's Digest to look at. And spend her time at the front of the class with the other students giving them their lessons and working with them.

We had this little girl about my age, her and her family were from Hungary and didn't speak English. So my teacher at school put me with her to help her. Don't ask me why. But I remember that I was a feeler. I could feel peoples pain. I would look at their face and see it. My mother had a lot of pain. My mother left home when she was 15 years old, and never went back. Through the years my mother and I would fight. But I would never hold anything against her. For some reason I just had that feeling, I knew her hurt. So I tried to be loving and understanding, but through the fights we had, my sweet mother and I would not agree. The only thing I knew about my mother is that she left home at 15. She said she had brothers and sister. Her father was a Baptist preacher and he drank all the time. I do remember her saying that he used to beat her occasionally. Before my mother died she did tell me that she used to have a pony that she love dearly.

When I was a little girl growing up, my loving mother was gone all the time working and trying her best to raise and support us. I do remember all the times that I struggled with my reading. I used to transpose letters and numbers. I discovered later on in life that the issues I'm dealing with to this day, has a name. And it is called Dyslexia.

Dyslexia is a learning disorder characterized by difficulty reading due to problems identifying speech sounds and learning how to relate them to the letters and words. Also called specific reading disability dyslexia is a common learning disability in children. Dyslexia occurs in children with normal vision and intelligence. Sometimes dyslexia goes undiagnosed for years and isn't recognized until adulthood. If I remember correctly I was around 22 years old and I found out that I was born left handed and forced to switch to right-handed. At the time I had a full-time and a part-time job. For my part-time job I waited tables and the lady that I work with asked me,

"Diane are you left-handed?"

I said, "No, why?"

She told me that when I serve, I serve left-handed. So I asked my mother about that the next day and she told me yes, when I was a little girl she kept on smacking my hands and force me to be right-handed. I said OK! And I never thought too much more about it until later on in life.

So with my full-time job that I had, I worked at the company for 34 and half years. And all through the years I still struggled with my reading that nobody knew I was having. I would take private lessons trying to learn my phonics so I could sound out words. Occasionally on some of the special television programs that I watched, they had people that had learning disorders. People that were dyslexic. Talk about the brain and how the brain works right brain verses left brain. And asked myself

What the hell are they talking about? As time went on I finally caught on and I realize that I've had these issues all my life and being forced to be right-handed really didn't give me any favors because it created a lot of learning problems as well. Remember when I told you that I used to really stutter when I was a little girl. I forgot to mention that I also had a problem with swallowing. One of my visits to the dentist, the dentist told me that I had a reverse swallow and that he could teach me to swallow properly. Sometimes when I speak I can't get the words out clear enough because it rolls in my mouth and people have a hard time understanding me at times. I told the Dentist no, and what I've learned through the years. I really should have agreed for him to teach me to swallow properly it might of helped. God only knows but I am very blessed to be right where I am today.

Thank you God.

Come to find out that from being forced to change hands from left to right, created more learning issues for me. But for some reason, don't ask me why but I've always felt that I came into this world with those issues. That I had to overcome and work with them. So I never really put the blame on anybody. I don't know if my mother ever really knew, if she did she never said anything. All I know is that my mother worked all day in and day out to help raise her kids and I feel so blessed I had such a loving mother. With my mother working all the time, I never really saw much of her so I somewhat raised myself.

I remember when I was in the first grade I had this little boyfriend he knew that I was struggling with my reading. He said what are you going to do when the teacher calls on you to read I told him well I'm just gonna fake it. He says I hope you don't get caught. I can still see that little boy's face today. To this day I still have issues with my brain and trying to make out the sounds. And what there's supposed to say so my brain is still working right brain or left brain I don't know but I'm happy it is what it is to say

Thank you Jesus, thank you God for everything that you do for me.

When I was a little girl I went to church. I believe I started going maybe when I was 8 years old and I continued going by myself. Then I started asking questions. The questions that I ask my teachers, they couldn't answer and I became frustrated so I quit. I always knew there was something wonderful out there. Thats where the knowing comes in. As I said earlier, I can feel peoples pain.

I had been always a person that's been for the underdog so to speak. When I was in junior high school I was with some girls in gym class. We had a girl in our class that wore a set of falsies one day to school. On that day, one of her falsies fell out of her bra and we were in the locker room changing our clothes getting ready to take our showers and get ready to go to her next class. So when she was in the shower we hid her falsies. She came out and seen they were gone and the look on her face broke my heart I felt so bad I told that we had hid them and where she could find them. She started to cry. I ask myself today how that poor soul is doing and the impact that we had placed on her life. And whether she was able to move on. That was the last time I went out of my way to hurt someone for fun. I believe I was 13 years old. I had to learn that lesson.

Looking back on my life and some of the things I have done. It's gave me a better understanding why I felt I was born old. Some people say I am a old soul. I spend a lot of time alone. And I have found that I've always spend time alone which makes me a somewhat of a loner. I have found you have to like yourself before anybody else can like you. You also have to learn to love yourself and respect yourself. And be true to yourself.

Moving ahead in my journey. So with all the reading that I've done the last 12'years that I started my journey my spiritual journey I have found what my belief systems are. I do believe that we plan our journey when we can down to earth. I have gotten interested in astrology some what and what I've learned and what I've read that are natal chart tells our whole life story from start to finish. In our chart we have a lot of free space free will. It tells us about our mothers and fathers brothers or sisters what type of relationships that were going to have what are interested are in a just basically tells your story as a person is not telling what you can not do.

I have found that there is a blend of the God center, Christ conscience and the Holy Spirit. You can't have one without the other. I do believe incarnations and afterlife before and after. I do believe in light and dark energy. I have learned to love and live from the heart, which I call my God center and I tried to listen to that small voice just talking to me, which I call my God source and if you listen, it will never steer you wrong. I tell people that my truth isn't necessarily your truth and that's what matters. And your truth to you is what matters to you, this just how it works.

I am a great believer in angels, I believe I've had angels all my life but I never really recognize them until later on in my life. I did see a angel when I was around 13 or 14 years old.

With some other kids up on this hill and it was dark there is a cave on the edge there and we was with some boys as well. A few of us girls had to and make a potty run so he walked up the hill and looked up and lord behold there this huge angel it must've been at least 8 feet tall and it was hovering off the ground about 3 feet and it was shining brightly and it was coming down very steadily towards us. We ran back towards the cave hollered at the kids there told him to look around to see the angel some of them did we slid all the way down the hill on our butts to the road below and when we looked up the angel of us standing right on top of the cave. I can still see that in my minds eye.

I have learned through the years that when one is speaking about their beliefs that we have to be careful speaking of how we say things, everybody around you has there own belief system and we need to respect their feelings and how they feel and you don't want to be too pushy. Hopefully you can have an open discussion and who knows, what you say or they say may give you a spark and give you food for thought because there is always something to learn.

I told you earlier on that I've always been somewhat of a feeler. I guess because all my struggles that I had when I was little girl helped me to be the person I am today. I always want the best for everybody. I look around and I can see peoples eyes and I ask God to bless them every day. I've been known to help people I see on the side the road with a sign stating that they needed some help. I once saw a sign that a lady had, saying they were collecting money so they could get this dog and train it.

Her husband had returned from the Iraq war and had issues, so they felt if they had a service dog, that it could give him some comfort, so they needed so much money to the train the dog. I stopped by and gave her a check for the full amount of what she needed. She broke down in tears. I told her "Sweet girl don't worry, everything will work out for you." A couple weeks later I got a phone call from her, she had told me that her husband had left town, left the state and was not interested in having the service dog. She wanted to give me most of the money back, she said she couldn't get it all back to me but she could give most of it. The young girl, who also had her son with her, were both stranded here in St. George, Utah they came down from Salt Lake

City. No job, no money, I told the young girl to keep the money, hoping it could help her get on her feet with her young son.

Don't ask me why I do this, it just happens occasionally. I guess it's just part of my personality and the things in life I'm supposed to be doing.

I was just thinking of when I said, I don't know why I do this. Well, looking back when I was a little girl, about four years old, my mother had three kids and was on welfare. It is Christmas Eve and I asked my mother where is our Christmas tree, everybody has a Christmas tree but us. My mother said Sis, she always called me Sis,

"Don't worry when you get up in the morning, there will be a Christmas tree."

I said, "OK" and went to bed.

Got up the next morning and yes there was a Christmas tree! It was beautiful, there were toys and presents all over and there was food on the table so we could have something to eat for Christmas. It seems for the last five years or so, I always refer back to this Christmas, when I was four years old. And it makes me feel so blessed. So when I do things for people I do it from the heart and just say

Thank you God for giving me the means to do this. I feel that we need to help one another and to help pick up each other when we are struggling. We all need help from time to time, may it be a helping hand, a smile, or somebody just to listen and hold your hand.

I told you earlier on, that I would talk more about my Richard. When I started writing this book For Anne Deidre my Richard found out that he had lung cancer. So I had to put my book on hold so I could take care of him.

I had talked to Anne, who was such a loving angel.

She said "Diane, you take the time that you need."

I did take the time. My precious Richard only lasted six weeks. Tomorrow, May 21, 2016 will be four weeks that he has passed on. It was so hard to let him go, but I had to. I couldn't watch him suffer anymore. I have never seen anybody go down the rabbit hole that fast. But I know he is in a better place, he is getting ready for his next adventure. Towards the end I was talking to him about the angels. There was one time earlier on when he didn't believe in angels.

He would say, "I don't want to talk about angels."

I said "OK." But I kept on talking about the angels.

It was the last couple weeks before he passed, that I was talking about Angels.

Richard said, "Yes the Angels."

I knew that he was getting ready to make the transition, he was doing a lot of talking to himself and I just had that gut feeling that they were preparing him on the other side to take him home. I did talk to him about his late wife Jean. I told him that I had asked her to come and take him home. The day that he passed

I said, "you know your angels are here.

And he said, "yes, I know they're here.

"I asked Jean to come and get you."

And he said, "Yes."

He stated that Jean told him that she was coming for him.

I said to him, "what a wonderful blessing! And I am so happy for you."

I laid down beside him, I gave him a big hug and he gave me a big hug and we kissed. It's was our last kiss. I am so blessed that I was able to have this loving soul in my life. So I asked God every day to please take care of him. I was so happy that he was finally able to connect with the angels.

Thank you God, thank you Jesus, thank you Archangel Michael, thank you Archangel Rafael. Thank you to all of my angel team and all my guides.

And all my beautiful friends that I've met throughout the years and the lovely people that are helping me get over my pain. I asked my angels to come into my sleep at night to help me heal.

I love this saying that I found on a wall in our local hospital.

May I be in peace.
May my heart remain open.
May I awaken to the light
which is my true nature.
May I be healed.
May I be a source of healing
for all beings.

Alara Canfield

After suffering in silence for over twenty years, Alara Canfield realized that the entire world she had created did not align with her true joy and happiness. She decided then and there she would have to change her life no matter the cost. Over the past 7 years, Alara has left her marriage and found true love; she left her government job and now is making a difference globally doing what she loves and being of service to her community and the world.

Alara is a transformation consultant and catalyst for change. She is a speaker, author, intuitive healer, life coach, and host of The Alara Canfield Show—

Awaken To Happiness Now Global Series.

Alara uses her intuition and energy mastery to help her clients align with the truth of who they are as powerful beings here to experience their greatest, prosperous, and radiant life. She is able to transmit vibration and frequency in order to transmute energy that is not serving her clients in order for them to be in greater alignment with their soul's purpose and shine in the world.

Alara is on a mission to inspire and self-empower you to live authentically with joy, ease, and love through a connection with Spirit and to realize your full potential, live the life of your dreams, and access happiness in every moment. She believes that life is meant to be happy and filled with joy, light, and laughter. It is time to BE who you truly are. It is time for you to SHINE!

Are you ready to awaken to happiness now?
Are you ready to shine your brilliance?
Are you ready to be your Radiant Self?

May I be in Peace

Alara Canfield

People say that sometimes change comes in an instant, in a split second. Can you imagine that a random movie, or a random scene in a movie, could change your life? Can you imagine that something as trivial as that could change the trajectory of your life, and the life of those closest to you?

It definitely did for me, and totally unexpectedly, and with such force that it could not be stopped.

So, what made me ask for a separation? What made me choose to end a marriage of almost 18 years? It was a movie, actually it was a scene in a movie. I was watching a movie in the theatre with my daughter, it was a romantic chick-flick. Why were we watching that? That alone makes no sense. During one scene when the main characters were on the beach, laughing, joyful, and happy, something happened in my heart chakra. I cannot say exactly what it was, but it wasn't pain or anything like that. There was a significant sensation in my heart in the middle of my chest, and I remember thinking and feeling,

I want that, I don't have that, I deserve that.

It was like my soul was talking to me, and saying that I was worthy of being happy and being loved, and loving someone else. You could say that was the beginning of the end of my marriage.

Suffice it to say, that when you choose something for your highest good from your heart, it turns out to be good for everyone involved. It took me a long time to learn that and accept it in my heart. So now, I choose from my heart for my highest good and for the highest good of all.

As I think back to my wedding day, so long ago, the signs were clear, but I didn't pay attention to them, I didn't want to see them. I had committed to this and I was going to go through with it. I was in my wedding gown, ready to go down the aisle with my father at my side. My head and heart were screaming to God, the Divine, anyone who could hear my inner plea,

Please send me someone to take me away from this!!!"

When the wedding music began and we started to walk down the aisle, I knew it was too late, and my heart sank, I could hardly breathe. When it was time to say my vows, I couldn't get the words out. I started crying softly. As the minister handed me a Kleenex surreptitiously, he said not to worry, this was just nerves, it would be okay. I cried through all of the vows, it was a sign, it was a premonition, it was a foretelling of the future.

Eighteen years later, I was finally taking a stand for my life, for my future, for me. I didn't know what the future held, nobody does, but somehow people, my family and friends, expected me to know how life was going to turn out. I didn't. I just knew that I had to get out of this marriage before it killed me. On the surface, it looked like I had it all. A good career, a loving husband, wonderful kids, 2-car garage home, a dog, everything but a picket fence. Now, to be honest, my now ex-husband, was not a bad guy. He was not violent, he was not knowingly abusive, in any way. I was just dying inside because I did not love him as I wanted to and he did not love me the way I wanted to be loved. He said he loved me.

I felt empty inside, unloved. I was tired. I was tired of the constant bickering and the constant negativity that radiated from him when we were together. I was tired of feeling like I had to walk on eggshells around him for fear that we would argue about something. He just didn't get me at all, we were not on the same page, heck we were not even in the same book.

For some reason, I felt like everything was always my fault, all of the problems in our marriage were my fault. Maybe because he never took responsibility for any of our problems. He didn't see them, he didn't acknowledge them, and he certainly didn't talk about them. We went to a psychiatrist once, and my husband didn't say anything during the meeting, and the doctor said that I was just depressed and prescribed anti-depressants. I felt like a depressed, ranting, crazy woman. And, no the sex was not good, even though we have 2 children, the sex was always very painful for me, and again he said it was my fault. I was too ashamed to see a doctor about it, but in hindsight maybe that would have helped.

When I asked him for a separation he was actually surprised. Well he was more shocked than surprised. He was more concerned about what he would tell his parents and friends than the effect it would have on our children. My kids meant everything to me then and they still do now. They are the only reason that I stayed in the marriage as long as I did. So many times, I tried to get out of it, but didn't because of the alleged negative effect it would have on the kids. I didn't want to ruin their lives. I think their lives would have been more adversely affected if I had stayed in the marriage even longer, a marriage that didn't work, where there was no love in the relationship, and where there was constant negativity.

What kind of example were they getting of a marriage and relationship? What kind of a role model was I being for them?

It is interesting that now, I am happier than I have ever been and I never took the anti-depressants. I am now married to the love of my life, living in Europe, doing work that is fulfilling to my soul. And, we have really good sex all of the time, no pain at all. So perhaps it wasn't all my fault after all.

And, this new happy life was a result of all of the choices that I made for myself in the last 7-8 years, since I chose to separate, listening to and following my own guidance. Working on myself energetically and emotionally, working with my spiritual team on a daily basis.

You can change your life too. You can consciously choose a better reality for yourself. Since I have been choosing in this way, my life has completely transformed in a magical and positive way. As my children see me making new choices for my life and seeing my happiness, it shows them the power of choosing from your heart.

I wish I would have made choices from my heart for my highest good earlier in my life. Surprisingly, I was married before. It is not something that I talk about often, but it seems relevant here.

When I was 20, I decided to go home to India for a visit, just for a few weeks. My parents were already there visiting, so it was the perfect time. My friends had joked that I had better not come back married. I laughed and told them no, I was just going for a visit. Little did I know, that on the same day that I arrived at my family's home in India, my future husband and in-laws were coming to meet me. Needless to say, it all happened very fast and very quickly.

Yes, I got married! Why? Why would I agree to an arranged marriage with a man that I did not know at all?

At the time, I was trying to be the good girl, doing what was socially acceptable. I thought I was doing the right thing, what was expected of me to please my father and the family. My father-in-law was a friend of my father's from his college days, so it was accepted that the family was a good family. Even though the question was asked of me of whether or not I wanted to get married, I didn't really feel like I had a choice. Although, I had no idea that I was going to meet my future husband the day that I arrived, obviously it was planned on their side. It is still common to have arranged marriages in India, and it probably does work for most people. But it definitely didn't for me or my sister who had an arranged marriage as well a few years before me. To be fair, it has worked for my brother, but then again his wife came from India. Perhaps there is a difference between North American men who marry Indian wives and North American women who marry Indian men.

Needless to say, it was a disaster. I was raised in Canada, so my values and upbringing were different than of the girls raised in India. But when I was in India, I was trying to be an Indian girl. It was messed up, I was messed up.

I was raised in a very conservative home with a lot of rules. My parents were very protective and a little bit controlling. I had to follow the Indian rules and customs as well as try to fit into the Canadian society and culture. I did not feel comfortable bringing friends home while I was growing up because I never knew what kind of mood my father was going to be in; he was an alcoholic, or a recovering alcoholic.

My mother was always working, so she was never home, and when she was, she was always cooking and stressed out. She and all of us were always walking on eggshells around my father, not knowing how he would react. And then, he started going to India a lot, and was never home, so my mother was working double time to make ends meet and pay for all of the expenses and take care of the house and kids. Not an easy life for sure, but it taught me to think for myself, or so I thought.

Everything seemed fine while I was in India, my husband was nice, my in-laws were very nice and caring. After I came back to Canada a few months later, I started the proceedings to sponsor my husband so that he could also come to Canada. It took about 9 months for my husband to arrive, I was so happy, I felt like our new life was finally beginning.

The day that he arrived was one of the happiest days of my life and by the end of the day one of extreme sadness and pain. And, this was just the beginning. I was very innocent, naive, and very sheltered growing up. I did not know that people could be mean for no reason, I did not know of the depth of cruelty that is really possible. I couldn't find any way to justify or reason out why he was so mean and cruel. Even now, as I think back, the only explanation that I can come up with is that he must have been really miserable and hated his life so he was taking it out on me.

I am not going to go into the nitty gritty details of the mental, emotional, and sexual abuse that I endured for over 12 months that truly shattered my perception of reality. It was as if the total foundation that I had built my life on came crumbling down around me.

I was ashamed and embarrassed by what I had become in only 2 years. I was ashamed and embarrassed to have experienced what I had experienced. I couldn't talk to anyone. I didn't want anyone to know what I was going through. I thought I had to suck it up and just endure it. I had made my bed and now I had to sleep in it, or that is the saying. Marriage was supposed to be forever, especially an Indian marriage.

What would the family say about me? What would society think of me? What would this do to my parents?

At one point during this marriage, I even attempted to end my life. I was so depressed, I felt so unworthy, I no longer had any respect for myself for letting myself get in this situation. My self-esteem and self-confidence were in the gutter. I could not see any way out of this situation. But the only thing that stopped me at the time was a thought that came into my mind and awareness.

The thought was *What would this do to Mom and Dad?*

I couldn't do it.

I went home even more defeated, more depressed. I couldn't even end my life! When I got home, I was still crying, still sobbing, still lost. I started praying to God, the Divine to give me some guidance, to help me out of this situation. During this breakdown, I had the most profound spiritual experience up to that point. I didn't understand it. It actually frightened me. But, I am grateful for it, for the experience, and for the grace and blessings I received in that moment, and from then onwards. That is one of the reasons why I have said time and time again that I have no regrets. If I had to, I would do it all over again, just so that I could have that experience, that blessing, that grace.

I did leave my husband eventually, and I only ever saw him once after that. When I finally made the decision to end the marriage once and for all, I didn't do it for myself, no, I did it for my younger sister. My husband said something to me that freaked me out and made me so angry, that if I had a weapon in my hand at the time, I would have killed him. My sister was 12 at the time, and he said that she was probably sleeping around with guys, that made me sick. How could he think such a thing? How was he looking at her? I ended the marriage finally to protect her. I was not worthy of protection in my mind, but my sister definitely was worth it. I made the conscious decision that even his shadow would not cross my path or my children's path, much later when I re-married and had children. I deprived myself of certain social gatherings and experiences because I was not willing to take the chance of having his energy, even his shadow, affect me or my family again.

I didn't realize until recently how much that marriage had affected my future. When I met my now current husband, yes, #3, all of my fears from my first marriage came up to challenge me. I worked hard to consciously, emotionally, and energetically choose a different path, a different way of being, a different life. I consciously chose not to let the fears from the past further affect my present and future realities. I faced the demons once and for all.

The demons were the beliefs that I had taken on as my own and that I let have power over me. The demons were the fears that I had that I would experience the horror again, or that type of horror again. I chose love over fear, love for myself, love of myself, and love from my now-husband. I chose to have a new experience in the unknown. I chose to have trust. Trust in the Universe, Spirit, God that I felt was guiding me and had guided me to my current husband. I chose to live in the present instead of the past.

We think we are choosing for ourselves all of the time. We think we are in control of our lives, our future, and our reality. *But are we?*

Or are we being controlled by our emotions, our wounds, our beliefs, and our past? When we are truly present, and in the now, there is no fear, there is no anxiety, there is only the now.

In the now, most likely, you are fine, right? So, what would it be like to be present and in the now more often? What would it be like to live in connection with Spirit daily? What would it be like to know that you are guided by Spirit and trust that guidance?

I have been blessed to have several spiritual epiphanies in my life and they have taught me many powerful lessons and they continue to teach me and show me deeper truths as I grow, expand, and evolve into higher dimensions of consciousness and awareness.

The biggest truth in my life is that I am loved unconditionally by the Divine, Universe, God, Creator, Spirit, Source, use whatever name works for you. And, so are you! I am worthy and deserving of whatever I desire just because I exist, and so are you! I do believe that there are some things that are planned before we incarnate in this life-time, and they will happen, but what is important is how we react to them, what choices we make around them, how we love ourselves and others.

It took me a very long time to realize that what I had experienced with my first husband, although not very good, was required to wake me up. My first husband had chosen to show up as that expression of meanness and cruelty to be of service to me, out of deep love for me, so that I would wake up. He was a catalyst in my spiritual awakening, and I am grateful for him and to him, and love him dearly for helping me to wake up. I am grateful to my second husband for all of our experiences and for giving me the space to grow spiritually, even though he was not interested in that at all. I am grateful for him because we have two beautiful children that we love dearly and am feel honored and blessed that they chose me to be their mother.

I am grateful for all of my experiences and all of the challenges because they have brought me to where I am now, here sharing my story with you. Are you grateful for all of the twists and turns in your path? Can you see the gifts and blessings that you received along the way?

I have deep love for my family, my friends, my colleagues, my co-workers, my clients, my community as they have shown me who I am and who I am not. They have held up a mirror to help me to see myself and who I was being from time to time. Sometimes I liked what I saw, other times I did not. They are all a gift and blessing, and I am grateful for all of them.

It truly is amazing how much my life has changed, how much I have changed, how much I have let myself be more of who I truly am. A Divine, Radiant Being of Light and Love. As are you! I now host a telesummit called Awaken To Happiness Now, which is just beginning its 13th season which in itself is a huge accomplishment. I now have moved officially to Europe to live with my husband after selling my home and everything in it in Canada. I came to Europe with 2 suitcases, ready for a new life. I have clients all over the world who I facilitate healing and transformation with so that they too can create the life that they desire through energy healing and life coaching.

My life is expanding more and more into the unknown, but with deep trust in the Divine and in myself. My higher self and my angels and guides are always supporting me and guiding me to greater expansion and greater awareness.

What does the future hold for me? I am not sure, but I know it is glorious because I am loved and supported by the Divine. What does the future hold for you? What do you desire?

Go into your heart space and ask yourself, *What do I really want to experience now?* And then be still and listen. Be open to the guidance, trust it, and take inspired action. Your dreams can come true, you can have it all, take it from me, mine have come true, I do have it all, and so can you!

Colleen Chanel

Colleen Chanel is an International Award Winning Continental Song Stylist, World Class Entertainer, Transformational Concept Song Writer, Recording Artist, Actress, Global Keynote Performer/Speaker, MBA, Co Creative LifeStylization Coach, Inspirational Author, Certified Esoteric Healing Facilitator, Certified Angle Reader, Certified Love Master and Illuminating Divine Singing Oracle.

Colleen has graced the International Stage as well as the Global Entertainment Business for over 25 years. This gifted chanteuse has been honored throughout the world with numerous awards in music, performance and multimedia entertainment while being acknowledged and sought after in the metaphysical, conscious business, keynote performance, healing and humanitarian communities.

Ms. Chanel is a native of California, although Colleen considers herself a "Citizen of the World." She received her BA from the University of Santa Clara and an MBA from the College of Notre Dame. Among Colleen's many academic diplomas and financial licenses, she is also an Esoteric Healing Graduate from the International Health Network, Certified Angel Reader and a Certified Love Master. Colleen Chanel has been an avid metaphysical student throughout her life and an Intuitive Visionary Life Stylization Coach after completing the Enwaken Coaching Program in 2012.

Prior to fulfilling her dreams in entertainment, Ms. Chanel was a successful Stock Broker, Investment Analyst/ Consultant for a prestigious Commercial Real Estate Firm in San Francisco. Currently, Colleen Chanel is recording her 9th CD with original continental songs in French, Italian and Spanish. She will be launching her new professional career as the "Illuminating Divine Singing Oracle" later this year sharing her mystical gifts, personal channeled readings and intuitive vibrational songs. Colleen is also continuing her global financial market education in Crypto Currency Certification at One Academy.

colleenchanel.com
email:colleenchanel@rocketmail.com

Joie de Vivre

LifeStylization in My Illuminating Key of C

By Colleen Chanel

—This chapter was a lifetime in the making...

An Intuitive Joyful
Heart ignited by
A Loving Visionary Soul
Inspired with The Magical Spirit of
"Joie de Vivre"
powerfully transformed
Decades of Intense & Chaotic
Multi Dimensional Challenges
into the now
Intuitively Evolving
Divinely Aligned
Universally Thriving
New Earth Renaissance
Woman of Love, Light & Joy

—Excerpt from Colleen Chanel's Forthcoming book:
Illuminating LifeStylization in Your Key of C
Creatively...Consciously...Compassionately

Joie de Vivre

Colleen Chanel

What does a creative young girl who plays passionately for hours alone in her pretty pink playhouse as a brilliant CEO of her own International Philanthropic Corporation and a successful innovative token woman Stock Broker/Investment Analyst M.B.A. and globally award winning sophisticated Chanteuse/Recording Artist and an Intuitive Illuminating Divine Singing Oracle all have in common?
Ta Dah…ME

It may come as no surprise that my life's signature heart song since birth was and still is *I've Gotta Be Me*.

My beautiful mother would describe my birth to others as Colleen, my little Almond Joy (her nickname for me), was quick and easy, she dropped out. I prefer to reframe her memory from my soul wisdom and belief to…

I consciously made my debut on beautiful Gaia with my innate *Joie de Vivre (Love of Life)*.

I was born into a devout Catholic family culturally Patriarchal and with sprinklings of Matriarchal surrounded by love while also including the follow qualities...

Laughter
Celebration
Social Advantage
Family Gatherings
Travel & Adventure
Educational Privilege
AS WELL AS
Narcissism
Enmeshment
Codependency
High Expectations
Progressive Ambition
Dysfunctional Loyalty

When I was in fifth grade my ambitious father, who I adored, was the proud owner of his new Ford Dealership.

It was so much fun to watch him "wheeling and dealing" in his own smooth and unique charismatic way. Within months, I was bestowed the honor of part time (or whenever I felt like it) the new position of Filer in Chief. And so with deep joy, my business career had commenced.

As Dad's dealerships grew, I was privileged to be actively enrolled in numerous extraordinary national training and corporate educational programs. FMI School became a welcome supplement to my boring high school curriculum. I thrived in the higher practical learning environment coupled with the socializing of seasoned professionals. It was the greatest business foundation for my M.B.A. degree and the variety of career successes that were to follow.

During my undergraduate years at Santa Clara University, I worked part time at a fun job as a customer service undercover shopper. I enjoyed creatively impersonating a variety of potential customer types. The substantial discounts afforded me to begin growing a quality professional wardrobe that was always a major part of my career plan.

The girls in my freshman dorm were all from very wealthy society families. They had attended prestigious private girl's schools. Needless to say, my public high school experience from a small rural town did not warm their elite hearts towards me. They also did not respond well to my constant flow of incoming calls from male admirers and friends. Our dorm had one pay phone per floor and soon my messages were not being delivered to me. Studying endless hours in the library, working, connecting with friends from other colleges and traveling with my parents frequently throughout my four years became my new college reality.

I was somewhat content. Everything changed for the best when I began graduate school at the College of Notre Dame. Even though I had changed my undergraduate Economics major to Humanities where I thrived in Italian Renaissance Art History/Language/Philosophy, I knew I would need to take all my missed undergraduate business classes while engaging fully in the M.B.A. program. Not a problem. I was thrilled to be in my own eclectic apartment, being productive and working with Macy's as a customer service undercover shopper for all the Bay Area stores that I had earlier submitted as a convincing proposal.

The M.B.A.. classes were mentally stimulating and I excelled graduating at the top of my class. My years there were the most consistently happy that I had ever experienced in my entire life to date. I was my own woman, healthy and intellectually confident while living in my own uniquely decorated sacred space including my precious animal friends…three fish, one turtle and two birds. I was HOME grounded in "Joie de Vivre".

I also met my handsome worldly future husband. He romantically courted me while wining, dining, dancing and enjoying memorable cultural pleasures of our beloved San

Francisco. Could life get any better than this after an elaborate wedding of my dreams?

Unfortunately, the Fairy Tale ended abruptly the night of our honeymoon. My husband became distant, emotionally abusive and a workaholic. During our brief marriage of two years, I did flourish as a successful stock broker and happily participated in a thriving women's professional community. My husband received a sudden promotion in a town that I had never wanted to live in since birth.

My soul intuitively knew that darkness, tragedy and sadness would engulf me. Even though I was at the height of my career, I reluctantly moved to a huge new house, not a loving home. I quickly transferred into an office that was highly dysfunctional yet luckily, soon after, I was offered a position with a smaller kinder ethical firm. It was a good decision until our office building burnt down unexpectedly.

Within a week, I realized I was pregnant yet lost my baby due to the enormous stress I was under. As they say, bad news comes in three's. My cold hearted husband came home to announce that he should not be married with no explanation or discussion. I was confused, devastated and in shock. I grew up believing that we were married for life in the Catholic Church. California is a no contest divorce state. It only takes one partner to file and your marriage is dissolved in 6 months.

Within a year of useless attempts by me to save our marriage, the papers were filed and I moved to San Francisco where I changed careers that would insure a stable salary. I became the first woman Investment Analyst for a prestigious East Coast based Commercial Real Estate Firm. Even though I had a great office, a beautiful shared apartment in the desired Marina District and a wonderful coworker environment, my heart was not in the work.

About a year later, my parents had purchased a charming summer beach house in Santa Cruz. As I was returning from my initial visit, a truck hit me head on and the driver was uninsured.

The horrific accident left me in unbearable back pain coupled with the inability to walk. I reluctantly moved into the summer house with a nagging intuitive feeling that something was not exactly right with the entire situation. Although the core family dynamics were not ideal, I was grateful to be safe and decided to end the long court battle of my divorce. I borrowed the significant funds to settle and pay off my mounting attorney debts.

Shortly after my decision, I bought a small singing machine (aka Karaoke machine) and began to sing every song that was filled with heartbreak, loss and grief while lying flat on my back in physical/emotional anguish. Within a few weeks, my entire body began to feel better and I was singing songs of love, joy and faith.

Divine inspiration followed. Since I loved to travel and my voice was better than average, even though I never had a singing lesson, my business mind inquired…

Why not create an elegant continental show and travel in Europe, the entire World? I asked myself…*What do I have to lose, I know business, hence Why Not?*

The universe conspired to work with me as soon as I declared my intention. Musical opportunities, promotional professionals and my first Musical Director unfolded magically.

Vern Bennet was my mentor, my metaphysical friend and my musical inspiration. He immediately recognized the singing talent I never knew I possessed. He excitedly introduced me to his wealth of knowledge, experience and expertise. I had found my soul's calling in life. After the successful debut of my first live concert with a professional quartet at the famous Jazz Kuumbwa Center, I knew in advance to maximize my investment. A live cassette tape plus video would provide me with the initial marketing tools I needed to move toward my European/World plan.

After hearing and seeing me in live performance on stage, my talented saxophone player revealed to me that he was an orchestrator and conductor prior to retirement. Bill St. Pierre had played with the all-time greats and recognized that my rare singing talent coupled with my natural stage presence should be showcased with an orchestra. Within a year, I had produced and performed a fully orchestrated show at the Coconut Grove. The Steinback Forum followed so I could primarily record a professional live video in a large world renowned venue with special lighting and staging.

At the same time, I had discovered that my parents' beach house I had been living in was actually mine. My parents intentionally did not tell me that my beloved uncle had lent them the money to purchase the house, with a binding handshake agreement it would be placed in my name as the owner. When confronted with the truth, my beloved trusted father looked me straight in the eye and said "You don't deserve it". No further explanation was provided as my uncle and I sat there in shock. I felt the sharp pain of complete betrayal and devastation. He was not budging and it would be a lifelong wedge between us until just prior to his death decades later.

I was determined now more than ever, to pursue my dreams, my life and disconnect from the illusion of a loyal unconditional loving family. With no money yet several credit cards in hand, I was off to Europe with my orchestrations from single accompaniment to full symphony. I began attending international musical business conferences, made contacts while learning the details and then showcasing my voice/performance talents after hours. My career blossomed, as did I for over 20 years.

I was fully embracing my life's soul mission and fulfilled that young girl's dream with "Joie de Vivre".

During the first 10 years, I had not had the best recording circumstances on the road nor musically aligned inspiration to record CDs. I finally met my perfect producer/song writer/musical director, Craig Brandwynne. He had recently moved from New York to Raleigh where a few months prior I had intuitively purchased my first home.

I loved creating concept albums with him. The entire recording and production experience filled my heart once again with "Joie de Vivre". We are currently on our 9th CD that will be released in 2018. Shortly after finishing my 8th CD, news of my mother's terminal illness took priority. I canceled all my international appearances and flew home to California. At that time her life expectancy was uncertain.

I knew that my parents and I had lifelong issues to resolve and no matter what had happened in the past, I loved them both deeply and unconditionally. I was grateful to be with them during their end of life. There was so much healing, laughter and tears between the three of us. We were blessed to enjoy each other for 3 more years.

My father transitioned within a few months after my mother's passing. I choose not to go into great depth for the several years that followed. It was my darkest night of the soul with remaining family, financial loss, foreclosure, homelessness, severe health challenges, betrayal, deceit, untruthful gossip, life threats that had me in protective isolation for years and more. Instead I will reflect on what I now know to be true and why my life has been blessed. In retrospect, my family was the ideal fertile foundation for an intuitive highly sensitive empath to grow, expand and reinvent, time after time, as the rising phoenix from all of life's challenges. Perhaps not always happy and easy, yet the rewards of becoming the authentic, loving, integrated woman that I am today makes it all worthwhile. I am grateful beyond measure.

My new life chapter has begun filled with renewed "Joie de Vivre" at a powerful higher consciousness level I have never experienced. Through years of traditional therapy, multiple energy healing and deep honest self-reflection coupled with all the human and nonhuman angels that have guided me through it all, I have been gifted this extraordinary journey and now...
I begin with a new peaceful song in my heart...

There IS Only...LOVE.

Within the last three years, I met my divine romantic soul partner, I have discovered the perfect blending of my spiritual, musical and intuitive gifts to share with the world plus I am moving to a new home in a new country with my handsome intelligent beloved fiancée' who loves to laugh, travel and passionately makes love with me. We have an entire new life to enjoy together. I know, without a doubt, that our love is all in divine timing with the conscious assistance of my inspired action. A few years back, I recorded an intentional divine soul partner song embedded with quantum energetic light and love.

Your Tenderness was so divinely aligned with my beloved, that as I recorded this beautiful song, I could feel the depth and power of his love prior to our meeting. On a last minute Caribbean Christmas Cruise, I met Dave the first night. We instantly became friends and by New Year's Eve we were engaged. For someone like me who has been engaged five times yet always managed to either sabotage or freely exit a wrong relationship, I just simply, quickly and honestly knew we belonged together. That has never changed to this day. He truly is my safe place to fall that all my life I knew existed yet never experienced. Yes, we do have our differences and at times the average frustrating adjustments.

We always ask each other "Is life better together or
apart? The answer remains the same...
"Together."

The other extraordinary miracle in my life was uncovering the essence of my soul's gift to the world. I had been struggling for quite some time until I entered the coaching program for this book.

Anne Deidre discovered this powerful and perfectly aligned calling as we prepared for her Intuitive Global Summit last year. I successfully debuted on her show as the "Illuminating Divine Singing Oracle." It was so much fun, natural, effortless and profound. I am deeply grateful for her intuitive wisdom and divine guidance. As soon as I comfortably settle into our new home after my upcoming marriage, I will be launching and offering my newly integrated gift globally.

Stay tuned… It has been an amazing writing journey to share this chapter that has indeed been a lifetime in the making and will continue to evolve into new exciting adventures.

My Summation…

Thee Best IS Yet to Come!

Nattalia Estar

Nattalia Estar was born in a little village nestled in a vast forest near Siberia, Russia. She left her home at the age of twenty in order to discover the important purpose that compelled her since her childhood. She pursued her career as a successful singer, traveling to many places throughout the world. Then only a few years into her journey she was faced with a devastating disease. During the next several years she struggled physically and emotionally, enduring countless and unsuccessful traditional medical treatments. With an overwhelming feeling of hopelessness, Nattalia left her singing career and embarked on a quest to overcome her condition. She finally found hope in holistic healing.

Her illness was healed. And even more importantly, she found a whole new world of deep inner spiritual transformation and connections to the higher realms. While she was looking for healing, she aligned herself with her true purpose of spiritual awakening.

Nattalia had become a student of metaphysical and esoteric arts. She has studied several different healing modalities and has earned various Certifications in alternative healing.

Today Nattalia is a spiritual teacher and energy healer. She is Certified Clinical Nutritionist, Certified Crystal Resonance Therapist and transformational retreat facilitator. Nattalia offers intuitive readings, personal distant crystal healing and group coaching programs. She supports people in inner alchemy while creating radical confidence and passionate living through courses, events, blogs and personal sessions.

Visit mytempleofhealing.com for our products, courses and services or email info@mytempleofhealing.com

Make a Wish Upon a Star

(My Journey From a Little Village of Russia to America and the World)

Nattalia Estar

I woke up from the cold, that was piercing my body through my skin and creeping into my bones. I fought it for a while pulling the thin blanket over my face but gave up and opened my eyes. I found myself sleeping in the car at the top of Mount Shasta, CA with a tapestry of stars hovering over me. *I haven't seen that many stars in so long*, I thought and started to remember how I got here last night. I remembered driving from Sacramento for four hours and going straight up to the top of the mountain. It was my first time driving a car alone by myself for the long distance and I was so proud of myself for overcoming fears of driving and surmounting yet another challenge and another mountain.

I grew up in Russia in a little village near Siberia with a population of about three hundred people. We never had a car in my family. I would ride to a kindergarten in a huge horse-drawn sleigh and my mother would cover me with a pile of hay to keep me warm in the merciless Russian winter. One morning it was still dark when she took me to the kindergarten and the horse man happened to be drunk as that what most men did in my village. He could not handle the horse and we got into a crush: the sleigh rolled over while I flew into the snow with the sleigh landing on top of me. My mother had to dig me out of the snow, while she cursed the horse-man for what he seemed to care less. She brushed off the snow from my crying frozen face, covered me with dry hay and we continued to the kindergarten like nothing ever happened. No ambulance, no therapy for terrified child that almost died under heavy huge sleigh.

The only vehicle I drove in my childhood was my father's tractor when we planted potatoes in a field during the Spring. My dad would go behind the plow and mom would follow him with a bucket of potatoes planting them for a new harvest. I was fourteen years old at the time and would proudly sit in my father's tractor feeling very responsible for helping to grow the food that we would rely on during the cold and long winter months. My family struggled with poverty and the only food we ate was that which was sourced from Nature. My mother would plant a garden every summer and I would pick tomatoes right before they fully ripened. I remember sneaking into my grandmother's garden and picking gooseberries, not yet ripe, when granny would spot me through the window and yell at me for not being patient in waiting for the berries to ripen.

In the summertime I would go to the woods and pick buckets and baskets of wild berries of all kinds: wild strawberries, blueberries and raspberries. It was my favorite time of the year because I could indulge in these sweet berries, which were the only sweets I got to enjoy as a child. Chocolate and ice cream was a privilege to the rich family's kids and berries were a treasure of mine. In the Fall there were cranberries and mushrooms and me and mom would bring baskets of those home. Mother taught me how to chose which mushrooms were edible and which were poisonous, then she would fry mushrooms with potatoes and make our most favorite meal. The wild food was a gift of a forest to its people, for the nature of Nature is always giving. Only humans are too blind to see it when trying to sub-serve Nature to its Ego.

I communed with Nature very intimately. I would go to a meadow of wild flowers where I would lay down and watch the sun sinking over the forest, waiting for the first gems of stars to appear in the multi-colored evening sky. And when the first star shine on me, I would wish upon that star, one day, I will go into the "big world" and travel all over the planet just like a super star.

I was artistic since birth and began singing on stage at the age of five. Singing and performing was very natural and easy for me to do.

Also, at the age of five I would tell everyone that when I grow up I will travel across the ocean and will live in America. It was a very strange thing for a small child to say since there were no cell phones, Internet, or computers at that time in our village. Our black and white TV had only two channels. I did not know much about America and for everyone else in the village this idea seemed impossible.

> They would laugh at me and say, "Yes, you'll go there in your dreams! Girl, your fate is the same as your mother's- milking a cow, growing potatoes and bearing children here in this village."

And there was a truth to that saying, as my dreams will eventually take me to America.

One night, I knew the time had come for me to leave my little world that I had known for twenty years. I graduated from college as a singer and an actress. The call of the "big world" beckoned and became all-consuming that I could not wait any longer.

I slipped through the door, I went on a road and stopped the big cargo truck that was going to Moscow. I did not have the money to buy a train ticket, so I begged the truck driver to take me to Moscow so I can make my dreams come true.

If there is something you want to do in your life and your excuse for not doing it is not having money-think again. All you need is you! Not having money did not stop me from following my purpose. I had the most important asset-myself, and I knew it was enough to begin with.

We never had money in my family as my father struggled with alcohol addiction, and my mother worked two low-paying jobs milking cows during the day and doing some heavy labor job at night. That was the other reason for me to leave my parents so I can help to get them out of poverty. I was twenty years old but I knew they would forgive me for leaving them this way, but it felt the right decision to make at that time. Twelve hours of laying on the back of a cargo truck was enough time for me to cry and grieve the life I left behind: my little village and my poor parents that I loved so much despite the violence and abuse. I always had so much compassion toward them and understanding that they were the victims of their own childhood abuse and were doing the best they knew how. But what I was bringing with me to my new exciting journey was the shame for my alcoholic father, inadequacy for growing up in poverty and deprivation, and low self-esteem that was destroyed during the school years through bullying and humiliation. For the rest of my journey, and up until now, I would be cultivating self-worth and self-love, overcoming my feeling of inadequacy, healing my childhood traumas, and learning to trust life and myself over and over.

The big city was very different from my little village. The job I got from an ad in a newspaper was to sell cookies and pre-made lunches on the street for two dollars a day. I was sleeping on the floor on a bunch of coats and I was eating the leftovers from the unsold part of the lunches. Even though I was grateful to have this little job as the opportunity door to a "big world", I felt there was something better for me out there. One day, I saw an ad in a newspaper for a singing position at a restaurant. I rushed to the audition as every cell of my body was saying "Yes!" My bold and courageous attitude shocked the management at the audition,

"So, what is your repertoire? Do you have a singing program?

I said, "I don't have any, as I shrugged my shoulders and added, "But I have a voice!"

The management looked at each other and asked,

"Can you sing something now?"

I was very happy to sing my favorite song, *My Heart*

Will Go On from the movie, *Titanic*, for it was the song that earned me many winning places at singing competitions back in the village.

After I was done the management affirmed:

"You definitely got the voice but the occupation requires repertoire, a program of songs that you will perform. Come back when you have it."

I went back to the street selling cookies and lunches, determined to get that program as soon as possible. In my spare time in between selling the lunches and washing the dishes, I practiced singing with a tape cassette player. I would save my two dollars a day to purchase the music for the songs and cassettes. I would practice singing and dancing, imagining myself performing on stage while holding my hairbrush as an imaginary microphone. I rushed to that restaurant with only four songs in my repertoire because the lunch business was failing and the lady was about to lay me off. The management was surprised to see me back that soon, but I stared at them with unshakable determination and firmly announced that I now have four songs in my repertoire and ready to perform on stage. To my own disbelief, I was hired. I sang my four songs over and over again every time new people would enter the restaurant. I danced and performed and shined like a star, shining the light of my soul out of my heart and into the hearts of my listeners, touching them in their very depth.

Sitting here on the top of Mt Shasta and watching the sun rising, I am recalling a time when I made another big leap of faith into the desert of the heating Sun and mysterious pyramids. It started with me going to Egypt for a week vacation. One evening I heard a band singing at the resort where I was staying. I missed to sing while on vacation so I thought to ask to sing couple of songs with the band just for fun. That is how I got offered a singing contract to work in Egypt for a whole year. On my return to Moscow I was overcoming my own fears and the negative chatter from friends and family about me being enslaved and exploited by the Egyptians. I thanked everyone for their concerns for me, packed up my suitcase and left.

The next two years in Egypt were the most remarkable years of my life. I sang in resorts, swam in the Red Sea and visited the Great Pyramids several times. After Egypt, I traveled to Spain and spent six months on a contract there. I worked all over Moscow in a high-end restaurants and clubs. I sang and danced with the joy, I was doing what I loved for a living and was well rewarded for my gifts and talents. I kept visiting my family every month and helped to end their struggle with poverty. I hired specialists and got whatever treatments were out there to help my father to overcome his alcohol addiction. I took my mother with me on trips to Egypt so she can also see the world beyond the small village she spent her entire life. I also started to work in an event-planning company managing several corporate events throughout Moscow. My career was blooming, and I was successful at making a comfortable living...until another crisis shook me off the top of the world and into the darkest night of the Soul, rebirthing me into a new and very different life.

My unresolved trauma from the years of violence, fear and abandonment longed to be addressed and demanded my attention through the physical illness that turned my life around. The diagnosis was obscure, more like a combination of system going out of whack. My hormones were badly unbalanced, my hair was falling out, I was gaining a lot of weight and a depression pulled me into the darkest void I had ever faced in my life.

In those darkest hours, I was tempted to take my own life and escape the pain and the shame of physical degradation. I had the most beautiful long hair in the village and had much pride of owning them. I could not stand the pain of loosing my hair and watching them fall out of control. I kept searching for a cure and was given a medication. They didn't know how to help me and weren't even trying to find out the cause of my disease. In my deepest and darkest hours I prayed to God for help and promised him that, if I got well, I would dedicate my life to God in whatever way it takes.

While searching for a cure I ran into an opportunity to travel and study in the United States. All of a sudden, the spark in my heart ignited the fire of a long forgotten dream. The knowing I had since childhood that I will be living in America flashed in my mind. My depression lifted as I hoped to find a cure for my illness in medically advanced country, I thought. I saved enough money from working all those years in the entertainment business. I quit singing and walked away from the stage into the land of opportunity with a hope for healing. It was yet another leap of faith I needed to undertake and another mountain to climb.

This big leap to the other side of the world—my life in America deserves its own chapter as it had presented me with new challenges or miracles for which to be grateful. I will save that for another book, perhaps. Learning English was yet another task I had to work hard at, so I can now write my own book in a foreign language that I am still learning every day!

In the following years, I would still be fighting my illness and going from doctor to doctor. They would give me one medication after another, but I am sure you've heard enough of those stories. I've been told that I was doomed to be on medication for the rest of my life in order to keep the illness suppressed.

That led me to begin the process of self-healing, searching and researching. I've changed my life style from clean eating to positive thinking. I understood that all the toxins begin in the mind mostly of emotional nature and then reflect in the body, as the body is the extension of the mind. I sought advice from alternative medicine, worked with herbs, crystals and plants. I was able to understand the cause of my hormonal imbalance was a reflection of imbalance of masculine and feminine energies within me. I had to cultivate and re-learn my divine feminine side that I was often unaware of. The world of Holistic healing pulled me in full, which resulted in aligning myself with something even bigger than my disease. When the illness left my body, there was no way for me to return back to the life I have lived before. I was changed.

Not only I healed my physical ailment, I was also able to resolve my childhood traumas, transmute the feeling of inadequacy and unworthiness into self-love and self-worth. I finally learned to love and accept my body. By being present in my body I explored every cell of my body with joy and felt my DNA in each cell as twisting, turning and expanding into a beautiful crystalline structure of light.

The lesson of self-love, however, is very prevalent in humanity these days. The religious teachings perpetuate unworthiness and guilt and have made it difficult for humans to love themselves. Now we are back to re-learning that by loving ourselves we are loving and honoring the God within.

Self-love is an essential component and a platform for healing to begin. I talk to my body with love, like I would with a little child. I ask it to forgive me for neglecting its needs and treating it carelessly. I dare to give myself what I have not received in my childhood from my parents - nurture and touch. I decided that I was worth it and started to take more time for myself and enjoy bubble baths with sea salt and essential oils and massages often. As I keep healing and taking care of myself, my desire to reach out and help others increase too.

Now sitting here on a top of Mt Shasta I got to lead my own healing spiritual retreat and help other souls overcome their difficulties.

I am now in my mid thirties. *Will I ever be challenged again in this lifetime?* I am sure I will be, but looking back at my previous experiences, I know I have all I need to overcome the challenges, perhaps now with more grace, ease and a spring in my steps. Those challenges brought me so much growth, self-knowledge and adventure that I would never had have I stayed in that little village.

I have recently lost a loved one, my brother that died in an accident. I found strength in me to overcome the pain of the loss and be the strong one to support my family through the grieving process. Past summer I took my mother on a trip to Egypt and Israel to cheer her up and pull her off her grieving mode.

Being extremely empathic I also have taken on her grief, but I decided to transmute this pain within my body and energy field because being an energy therapist I am now able to do it.

I also got into an abusive marriage that just ended while I am finishing up this book. Through this marriage, I discovered whole other layers of traumas I was carrying in my energy system that I had to release. After intense self-healing I walked away from the marriage in peace with my lessons learned and absolute unconditional love and gratitude for my ex-husband – my wonderful karmic teacher.

My life is not perfect, neither I claim myself to be a perfect person who knows it all and have a carefree easy life.

Yet I am here, I keep going and I am grateful to be alive. I am thankful for the opportunity to show up for my life lessons in this Earth school of life.

I have learned some of the important lessons my Soul came here to learn and experience through me: the lesson of courage by continuously letting go of what is secure and comfortable; the lesson of unconditional love by loving people without wanting them love you back or giving you anything in return; the lesson of deep compassion from experiencing pain and suffering in every cell of my body;

The lesson of gratitude for being grateful for it all.

Robin Grace

Robin Grace is an Author, Intuitive Empath, Teacher, Transformational Healer, graduate of the University of Santa Monica Soul Centered Living Program in Spiritual Psychology, Graduate, Certified Life Coach and featured author in the bestselling book series, The Inner Circle Chronicles.

As an adept energy master Robin receives transmissions in the form of words and feelings whereby she can translate profound information as she locates and powerfully dissolves blockages in your energy systems and auric field.

Growing up in a home deeply affected by her parents never coming out of their post traumatic shock of surviving the holocaust, she lived for decades in depression energy, fear and anxiety that was not hers but learned from her home life. But it wasn't until she had twins and her son was diagnosed as severely autistic, did she begin a journey seeking out both eastern and western medical information, homeopathic healers, master intuitives, and cutting edge healing methods. It wasn't long before her other twin presented in the shadows of autism and a diagnosis of bi-polar that healing herself and her children became her life mission.

bloomingblisswithin.com
or email : RobinGrace33@gmail.com

Today, Robin and her twins have overcome what seemed like insurmountable obstacles and are leading happy, productive lives. It is her joy to share with anyone interested in how you too can turn challenges into opportunities of growth and healing.

Now as CEO and founder of Blooming Bliss Within, LLC, Robin offers uniquely specialized personal readings, workshops, seminars, membership support programs for families living with Autism, life coaching and home study programs designed to empower her clients and teach them to be their own healers. It is her intention to help her clients break free from limiting beliefs and live the lives they came here to fulfill with more joy, purpose and fulfillment.

Also founded by Robin— *Heaven On Earth Productions* An innovative multimedia production company dedicated to creating, introducing and supporting original authentic conscious content.

Empathic Divine Magic

Robin Grace

My son was born listless and blue. Tears of joy welcoming his twin sister, who had just arrived perfect and wailing ended when a nurse whisked my beautiful baby girl from my arms and disappeared out the door. The steady beeping of a monitor silenced. I could feel my son slipping away.

The doctor pressed a button on a keypad by the door and within seconds the room filled with nurses and doctors. My sister who had been at my bedside, for hours, holding my hand was forcibly ushered out of the room. What was happening?

Till that moment I believed I was participating in the birthing of my babies when the reality hit me. I was not in control, but at the mercy of my physical body. I felt paralyzed, physically and emotionally. My breathing was labored, quick and shallow. I was gasping for air. A contraction burned through my core, and then nothing. No feeling. I didn't feel paralyzed, I was paralyzed. I couldn't feel anything beneath my chest, and without a doubt, I knew. These feelings of terror, feelings of suffocating, were not mine. I was embodying my son's experience.

I was in my baby's energetic field that existed outside of time and space as we know it and I was physically living his experience. Thoughts downloaded information fast. So fast I could barely keep up. I had experienced this type of transmission many times throughout my life from other people, but the transmissions were fleeting, and would leave as quickly as they arrived.

This was different, this was my child dying inside my body. I have no words to describe the determination my will had to birth him into the world. I was literally wrestling with his life force. Like flash cards with bullet points, information downloaded.
Had his sisters crying frightened him? Yes. Did her birth hurt and did he feel it? Yes. Had he changed his mind about coming into the world? Yes. He was leaving.

He decided *Oops, I've made a mistake, going home.*

His decision filled me with rage, it felt factual, emotionless, completely disconnected from my love of carrying him all these months and the miracle of life we would experience together.

My inability to breath brought me back into my body consciousness. It felt like bricks were being stacked on my chest. My son was not receiving oxygen and I had become one unified field of energy with my baby. He was suffocating and so was I. The crowd in the room responded quickly, everyone on purpose. No talking, no emotion.

A cart rolled up bedside preparing for an emergency C-section. My doctor approached with forceps. Calm and matter of fact he explained what was happening and why. His mouth moved. I knew he was speaking but I could not retain the information. I picked up sound bites. Something about forceps, a C-section, the placenta detaching from a wall. What wall? What are you talking about? I didn't care. I could feel my baby's life force slipping away. I saw the forceps. They were huge, barbaric, metal claws, like something the marquis de sade invented. I absolutely knew the forceps would bruise my baby, harm him in a way that would never be fixable. I panicked and what happened next was extraordinary and did not come from me.

I had been in the hospital the last four months of my pregnancy on total bed rest with bathroom privileges because I kept going into pre-term labor. My muscles had atrophied significantly and I had very little strength to push anymore and was already beyond exhausted. I truly believed if my baby was going to die, so would I. My doctor was about to insert the forceps into my body and I screamed

"NO!"

And that is when a force moved into my body. A powerhouse surge of energy moved through me, entering through the top of my head and in one solid jolt, my baby shot out of my body. My doctor caught him midair like you would catch a football. I hadn't taken a deep breath. I hadn't bared down to push. I had nothing to do with this delivery and I'm pretty sure Tom Brady wasn't hanging out in my vagina. Was it just adrenalin? The kind of energy we hear about that enables parents to lift cars off their children? A chemical response allowing a lover to lift a truck off their beloved? Or is this how God works? Is this how angels work through us? Is this our true spiritual ability? Can we request, access and anchor energy at our command? Would I be small about it later to myself, my children and dismiss this birth to science? Tell my son the story of his birth as having nothing more to do with saving his life as an adrenalin rush? Why would I do that?

So, I wouldn't have to face what it really was. That we are not in charge and when we consciously acknowledge this truth and claim that we are light source creation, we can access its infinite power. And when we acknowledge it is our birth right as divine beings having a human experience, we can create anything we can imagine.

> ***Our deepest fear is not that we are inadequate. Our deepest fear is that we are powerful beyond measure.***
> **– Marrianne Williamson**

The undeniable physical experience during my sons' birth left me with many unanswered questions. But more than that, the experience left me with an absolute knowing that what is invisible is more essential to our existence than anything in the physical world.

My twins were birthed four weeks pre-mature. During delivery my son lost seventeen seconds of air and weighed four and a half pounds. He was revived and breathing on his own but never cried or made a sound. I knew something was not right. I could feel it, sense it and see it in his eyes.

After three days in the hospital I was discharged with my daughter but her brother remained in the neo-natal unit because he had lost weight, he wasn't swallowing and required gavage feeding. It felt absurd when I thought about all the weight I had lost and gained in my life at will and fashionable punishment and my baby had only four pounds sustaining his life. Gaining weight was literally a matter between life and death.

My daughter continued to thrive and had a couple octaves Pavarotti would have been jealous of. She was magnificent. I spent hours gazing into her curios big blue eyes.

When I held her, she felt solid, powerful and opinionated. I know, how can a baby have opinions? Well, she absolutely did and I don't know how else to explain it other than she was an old soul. She refused to breast feed. Not only would she not latch on, she'd purse her lips and turn her head as far away from me as possible in disgust.

I felt like I was failing miserably as a mother. I ended up having to use a breast pump which I threw out a second story window of our house after experiencing its suction and I was sure I was going to lose a lung. Pumping hurt beyond what I could handle. What I couldn't handle, what I didn't know how to handle, was the numbness I felt when I thought about my son in the hospital. I suffered tremendous guilt over the natural flood of joy I experienced with my daughter and the numbness I felt when holding her brother. What was wrong with me? I was ashamed and told no one.

My family visited the neo-natal unit daily where my baby remained for a month. When I held him, the memories of his birth came flooding back, still vivid in not just my thoughts but my body. I'd immediately well with tears, my throat and chest would tighten and I felt intense fear and remorse. I wish I could make a great joke here, something about buyer's remorse and why don't hospitals have a return policy, but even my humor that had saved my sanity my entire life had lost its will.

When I held my son, I could feel his resistance to living. I felt helpless and devastated. Was I feeling his regret for incarnating? Yes. Did he believe he made a mistake? Yes. I could feel his will disconnected from his body. I could feel his energy, his life force outside of his body. He was checking out the world he was forcibly gatewayed into still refusing to be part of it. I would leave these visits an emotional wreck. I'd sit in my van and ball my eyes out, heaving sobs that eventually settled into a state of numb depression. And even though I had been in and out of long bouts of depression my entire life, this was different. This wasn't about me. This was about the rest of my son's life and I could feel something was not right with him and my inability to connect with him, comfort him, tell him no matter what, everything is going to be okay, left me in a place of indescribable helplessness.

Then one afternoon, in the fourth week of my son being in the hospital, a feeling washed over me similar to the jolt of energy that passed through my body during delivery and I just knew, I had to bring him home.

I will never forget this day. One of the nurses had knitted my son a cap and mittens so he wouldn't lose body heat. The yarns were bright florescent rainbow colors, something a teenager might wear skiing and SNAP! I saw a picture in my mind's eye of my teenage son snowboarding without a jacket.

And I thought, *OH MY GOD this kid is going to ski one day and why isn't he wearing a jacket?*

It wouldn't be until eight years later that I would learn the meaning of this vision and that not wearing a jacket, cold not affecting him, was a foreshadow of things to come. But that was how feelings and visions translated as information in my life.

I became overwhelmed with joy. A sliver of divine light snuck into my heart planting hope and possibility. I held my uncompromising position against the neo-natal teams' efforts to dissuade my decision and I took my son home.

However, even with the support of the invisible force of feeling and knowing within me, I was a nervous wreck. On the ride home from the hospital I noticed for the first time and what would eventually show up as a form of turrets, was the occasional flinching of my son's facial expression and jerking movements in his arms and legs. He was very weak and although he breastfed, it was exhausting for him and he'd fall asleep before he consumed enough to sustain him. I could go into the details but I don't really want to revisit searching for the breast pump in the bushes, so let's just leave it at, it still worked.

And pump I did. For an entire three months at which time the flesh around my nipples was cracked and raw and the pain went beyond my threshold of what I could tolerate. I cried. I cried a lot. I knew breast milk was invaluable to my sons' progress and I was determined until my doctor prescribed a cream with lanolin to repair the cuts and I had an allergic reaction to it. So, add itching, burning and swelling to raw torn bleeding flesh and that's accurate. This time I took the pump back to the hospital and donated it for another brave soul I prayed would have the spirit of a warrior and put me to shame.

At our first doctor appointment my son hadn't gained weight. I was instructed to feed him every three hours which translated into me being awake every three hours around the clock for two weeks, which turned into seven months. At our next doctor appointment my pediatrician was not negotiating and I did not argue. If in two weeks' time my baby had not gained weight he would return to the neo-natal unit. Two weeks later I returned to the doctor's office, severely sleep deprived, depressed and in a constant state of emotional reaction. If our dog barked, I jumped. If the doorbell rang, I screamed. A wasp had flown into the van on the way to the doctor's office and hovered around the twins. I swerved off the road and jumped out of the car as if a lion was about to eat my children. I had lost it. That last bit of rational discernment that accompanies people who get sleep was gone.

Thank God, my son had gained weight. I sobbed at the news and my pediatrician handed me a card of a psychiatrist he highly recommended for some additional support. Great. I presented in need of psychiatric help when I instinctively knew all I needed was a wise experienced mother and extra help at night so I could get much needed uninterrupted sleep.

I saw the psychiatrist once. She let me talk for two hours, didn't charge me and told me I was a typically depressed intelligent thirty-year- old new mother of multiple birth premature babies and that once I got the swing of motherhood I would be fine and the depression would lift.

Nope.

The depression lasted two years. During those first two years my daughter thrived typically reaching textbook milestones and her brother thrived to the rhythm of his own unique blueprint. He didn't cry until he was eight months old and taught himself to walk at nine months by pulling himself up to standing on anything he could grasp. The sofa, the staircase railing, curtains, and our dog. As if telepathically summoning our brilliant Greater Swiss Mountain dog, Benny, my son would latch onto Benny's fur and together they would lumber and stumble around the house.

Benny was heaven sent. He stopped our house from burning down three times. Not once, but three times. I would cook oatmeal in the middle of the night when feeding the babies and forget about it. We were renting an old house with a wood log country style cabin kitchen. The oatmeal would eventually dry out, catch flame and burn the ceiling wood beams. God bless Benny. As soon as he smelled smoke he would race upstairs, grab my bathrobe at my wrist and pull me to where I could see the smoke billowing up the staircase.

Benny didn't only stop the house from burning down. I had a phobia of spiders and Vancouver, where we were living, had spiders the size of your hand. Spiders with fur, a postal code and luggage. I'd often see them outside but never in the house. One night I was sitting in a glider chair feeding my daughter when I noticed one of those massive spiders just a few feet from me on the floor. I didn't scream. I had my baby in my arms and my protective mama bear instincts didn't let me. I imploded. Within seconds as if I had screamed at the top of my lungs, Benny came racing upstairs, charged into the room, located the spider and devoured it in seconds while looking directly into my eyes as he chewed.

Don't even try to tell me energy does not transmit emotion and information. I hadn't made a peep. I have no patience for skeptics or scientific dismissal of what is my reality and operating system of my existence and what eventually provided the information and path to assist, modify and dissolve many of the qualities that would soon make my son's life extraordinarily challenging.

When the twins were three years old work moved us from Vancouver, British Columbia to Fort Lauderdale, Florida. The seven- hour flight to Miami airport was a nightmare. My son screamed from the moment we entered the airport in Vancouver until we got outside of the Miami airport. His screaming upset many passengers and flight crew. Even the Captain came out to see what the problem was. My daughter told me the sound of the engine was hurting his ears. It must have been excruciating for him because he wasn't crying, he was screaming with every breath. High pitched screeching with every breath. I cried the entire flight. Passengers got angry at me. Several banned together and demanded I give him Benadryl, check his clothing, and change seats. One women lashed out at us

"Just fucking hit him till he stops already."

We were moved to the front of the plane and my daughter who wasn't disturbed in the least told me, it would all be over soon. By age three I knew my daughter was a clear clairvoyant consistently spot on with her predictions and information about people and events. At the age of eight she blurted out casually at dinner one night that I would be divorced when that reality wasn't on my radar yet. I was divorced several years later. She was also an invaluable part in her brother's evolution in that they had their own language and she would translate his needs when he became non-verbal at three years old.

Upon arriving in Florida, I enrolled the twins in a nearby preschool program and I unpacked our home. Before the end of the first week, I was called into the principle's office because my son had thrown a chair at a classmate that split the child's lip and the injury required stitches. In the dismissal meeting his teacher asked me if I knew what autism was. Like most people at that time I associated the question with Rain Man, the movie starring Tom Cruise and Dustin Hoffman who plays his older autistic brother.

I laughed. "You mean as in the movie?"

She ignored my comment and advised me to have my child evaluated ASAP because I didn't want to miss the window of early intervention. She went on to explain how crucial early intervention was to the quality of my son's future.

This was my introduction to being consumed with the race against time. Losing time meant losing my child to autism. I left the meeting and could not remember where I parked my van. I emotionally unraveled as the dots connected and that haunting knowing that had stayed with me since delivery was becoming an identified reality. I found my van by hitting the panic button and followed the alarm which felt appropriate to becoming unhinged. I put the twins in their car seats, got in the van and pulled out into oncoming traffic. Cars came to a screeching halt, horns sounded and I just kept driving unfazed that I could have just killed us all. I was in shock. Everything I felt since delivery was confirmed.

In 1997 my son was diagnosed as severely autistic by the head of the Behavioral Psychology Early Childhood Development Center now the Mailman Segal Center for Human Development at Nova Southeastern University in Davie Florida. I was told he was a textbook case. He had lost what little language he had and completely stopped making eye contact with anyone. My son as I knew him disappeared into something that I could feel took him over and no one knew the way out. Yet. I could feel he was trapped in something that made him unhappy, frustrated, and angry and he expressed it through self-harm and raging.

The Behavioral Diagnostic Psychologist and the leading pediatric neurologist specializing in autism at the Dan Marino Foundation, after observing my son for less than three minutes told me, he would never pass the maturity of a thirteen-year-old, he would never have friends, intimate relations and would never be an independent adult. He ended the appointment by telling me I was not equipped or skilled in early intervention strategies and that it would be best for our family that I put my child in an institution for preschool aged children with autism.

Upon hearing these words, I felt that familiar NO! But I pushed it aside allowing a lab coat, medical credentials and my emotions to override my intuitive information. I mean, what if I was wrong? I could never betray my child by not considering all possibilities.

I continued to seek, research, learn, study and stay abreast of eastern, western and intuitive quantum and energy medicine. It took me more than a decade following my son's diagnosis, following medical and clinical behavioral psychology protocols, trying intuitive healing modalities, many expensive and their outcomes proving less than effective, before I stopped dismissing my intuition.

My intuition was in tune with my son on multi-dimensional levels and when I trusted my information life improved. I toilet trained him in five minutes. I'll spare you the gory details leading up to this miraculous moment. But it was one of those days and I had had it. I hit break point when I couldn't stop gagging while cleaning feces off carpeting and just like that, information downloaded the answer. I did argue with spirit over this one because it started with telling me to go into the kitchen and get a bag of M&M's and I interpreted this as being meant for me. Like that was going to make me feel better? In an instant I knew otherwise. I found the bag and asked my son to come into the bathroom. I threw a red M&M into the toilet. It landed on the bottom and I told him to pee on it. Aside from him finding this hysterically funny, it worked. You can guess what blue was for and it worked like a charm along with giggles of delight at the entire game. I told our pediatrician about this one day and he casually said,

"Oh that's so creative. This is the same doc who told my son who refused to eat fruit at this time,

"Remember an apple a day keeps the doctor away."

To which then my eight-year-old son responded.

"That depends on how hard I throw it at you."

Against my better judgment I enrolled my son in the institution that operated under the public-school system. We didn't live within the geographic jurisdiction allowing us to attend. I packed up the house I had just unpacked, broke the lease and rented another home within the boundary limits. After six weeks of attending the program, I pulled my son out because his behaviors worsened and he displayed a wide variety of new symptoms that included but not limited to, endless screeching, dragging his knuckles on walls till they bled and staining his clothing, the carpets and curtains with the blood, spinning, banging his head on walls, hand flapping, repeatedly opening and slamming doors shut and spontaneous projectile vomiting. One month after taking him out of the program the institute was shut down due to a molestation case.

Now what? I needed answers and nobody knew anything more than applied behavior analysis (ABA) behavior modification programs, (that failed miserably) occupational therapy, speech therapy, experimental dietary restrictions, chelation therapy and an endless list of experimental vitamin protocols. None of these services were covered by health Insurance at that time and the urgency of early intervention being the difference between your child possibly evolving into an independent adult or doomed to a life of dependency was drilled into every parent of a newly diagnosed toddler with autism causing us all to live in a functional state of panic and financial hardship.

I was manic. I could not retain information or follow one thought to the next. The phone rang and rang and I refused to answer it. I was done trying to explain to anyone what I myself did not have words for.

I enrolled my daughter in a nearby day school where she began to make friends and have play dates. I made sure she had a full life outside of our home. For the first six months following the autism diagnosis I was consumed with my own grief when one afternoon something extraordinary happened while I was vacuuming the house.

The best way I can describe it was as if a veil was lifted from my awareness, my consciousness, like when you learn something and your life is different forever, and several things became crystal clear.

1 - If I lived in emotional reaction I did not have access to my intuitive abilities or innate wisdom. 2 - If I observed my son's behaviors without judgment or worry, the intensity of the behaviors lessoned and often extinguished. 3 - When I released myself of judgments that I was responsible for my son's circumstance his symptoms began to lessen. 4 - When I was happy my children were happy.

I have experienced firsthand; thoughts and emotions are energetic actions and they eventually manifest into physical form. I could fill my home with gloom and doom as simply as I could fill it with peace, love and joy. 5- And the greatest realization was that my suffering was how I was choosing to react to my circumstance and suffering had nothing to do with my son or autism. Living a life of suffering was my disease.

These realizations led me to address the long bouts of depression and subservience that were the pervasive backdrop of my entire life. I could no longer dismiss the impact of being raised by parents who never came out of their post traumatic shock of surviving the holocaust, had on my life.

By the age of five my daughter presented in the shadows of autism with severe learning challenges and a diagnosis of bi-polar and healing myself and my children became the focus of my life.

I began a journey seeking out both eastern and western medical information, homeopathic healers, master intuitives, behavioral psychologists, psychologists, spiritual healers and cutting-edge healing methods, like the QXCI and Indigo machines. I researched endlessly both scientific and holistic information and pioneering thought leaders in the world of autism and related issues.

Today, not only have these journeys awakened my understanding that we are each acutely responsible amidst any circumstance for how our behavior, our actions, our thoughts and intentions, what we say, and how we do or do not love ourselves affects others to the point where they become so severely emotionally disturbed and the disturbance perpetuates a chain of life disease that continues through our children suffering and future generations. Just like the disease of alcoholism is passed on from generation to generation, it's the same, just another flavor of diseased behavior. In coming to a deep realization of this as truth, I put an end to it.

Both my children have surpassed their prognoses, defied science, and are now living productive, joy inspired lives. Most people find it unfathomable to accept that our experiences, no matter how traumatic or chronically challenging, are simply invitations to awaken our intuition, super consciousness, and open our hearts to greater compassion and empathy.

Supported by mentors and my community of master intuitives and healers, words cannot capture the joy and fulfillment I receive being of service and experiencing firsthand how my life challenges and awakenings make walking the life path easier for myself, my clients, and all who I am and who I am not, aware of too! Be today as it may, it took me decades to arrive at this place of peace and fulfillment but it doesn't have to for you, the person reading this who may be walking through challenging circumstance, trying to survive day to day or feeling defeated having repeatedly tried and been disappointed at not making life changes that now seem impossible.

It is not hope I offer you, it is knowing. Knowing that you have everything you need inside to heal what challenges your peace and wellbeing. We all do. It is our divine birthright. And sometimes we need assistance discovering and remembering who we are and require guidance from those who have arrived to doing this work, to show us how. I know how because I did it and continue to. It brings me great joy assisting others as I have been.

Now as CEO and founder of Blooming Bliss Within, LLC, I offer affordable uniquely specialized three and five-day retreats, personal readings, ongoing membership support programs in the comfort of your own homes via zoom video conferencing, one on one and couples Holistic Life Coaching and home study programs designed to empower clients and teach them to be their own healers. It is my intention to help clients break free from limiting beliefs and live the lives they came here to fulfill with more joy, purpose and fulfillment.

In 2017 I founded, Heaven On Earth, Productions. An innovative multimedia production company dedicated to creating, introducing and supporting original authentic conscious content.

—Wishing you much love, light and laughter.

Also founded by Robin— *Heaven On Earth Productions*
An innovative multimedia production company dedicated to creating, introducing and supporting original authentic conscious content.

bloomingblisswithin.com
or email : RobinGrace33@gmail.com

Karen L. Jones

Karen L. Jones is a Psychiatric Nurse Practitioner, writer, educator, artist and "overcomer." You can read more about her journey in her upcoming book *Heart Eyes: An Intuitive Journey Through Cancer to True Love.*

For more information visit Karen's site
karenjonesnp.com
or email: karenljonesnp@gmail.com

Dreams

Karen L. Jones

Did they know why they knew? Not at all, but they knew!
–Malcolm Gladwell

Grandmom leaned against the wall in the bland, grey-white room listening to my aunt' earnest whispers. Grandmom looked over her shoulder, and into my eyes. She reached down into her blouse, pulled out her breast, and pointed at it.

I woke startled sweating into my sheets. The dream was so clear and real but this sweet dear woman had been dead since the 70's. The aunt in the dream was battling breast cancer. I knew what grandmom she meant. I called and made an appointment for a mammogram. I hadn't had one in at least five years.

From dream to mammogram, and then biopsy results, was a month. My unsuspecting mother was with me and heard the words,

"You have breast cancer."

Nothing can erase the feeling of numb agony that came as my breath went out of my body. Emotionally and mentally I slumped to the floor. In reality, I sat robot still in stunned silence in the bland, gray-white, exam room.

A suffocating Fear poured thickly over me. It came with the knowledge I was already a ghost that couldn't protect her mother from the words she just heard. My mortality was in my face, with images of the torturous, life-saving treatments sharpened the diagnosis but, it was the sudden loss of life-long dreams that penetrated my chest with a surgeon's knife.

Even at 43, I had still held onto the hope I would have a child. I had held onto this like a thumb sucking blanket soothing myself during a long haul of a deferred life. Waiting for love, waiting for good times. I seemed to have always waited.

"*God*, I demanded, "What do you want from me? Do you want me home? Is it my time now? If it is, I am ready to go!" The thought of staying was too harsh and overwhelming. Anything but chemo, my hair, my breasts, my feminine allure, and *power*!

What will I have, what do I have?

I had prided myself as a spiritual person, not overly attached to the physical! Note the word pride along with spiritual. At this point, I just wanted to check out. Not to die as much as not to have to deal with this scenario. According to Elizabeth Kubler-Ross' stages of grief, I was in flat out denial slipping into anger, swinging from numb to anger. These were my only emotions until, slowly, a balm of peace gradually seeped in. The first answer came. This was not my time to die and I would have to fight. I would have to dig deep within myself to surrender to this. Then, commit to a life that was mine to live, regardless of how horrendous, at the moment, it appeared.

Over several months I fasted, prayed and meditated. I fasted by eating a macrobiotic diet for cancer, which kept my rather large tumor from hurting but did nothing to reverse the size or hardness. I prayed, meditated, and dreamed. I kept a journal, to record questions, and the answers that came through the dreams, insights and thoughts about what I was going through. and what options I wanted versus what options I truly had.

A delay in treatment, surgical or otherwise, is never recommended even if on a macrobiotic diet. Time is cancer's friend. Cancer like poison ivy is easy to eradicate if dug up early. Once it gains a foothold with its deep tendril roots, it is a bear to remove. The surgeon who took the biopsy left several messages,

I am concerned that you haven't started treatment and wish to know what your plans are? I didn't return her call.

The fear of suffering chemo was intense. I needed to know what to do. I needed confidence, and mostly, I needed to brace myself for what lay ahead no matter what it was.

My prayers were more "crying for a vision." Like some Native Americans do when they "go up on the Hill" to meet with the Creator and find their life Path, I begged for visions, for the right choices and the right actions. Some answers to my questions came quickly, and some came slowly as a clear knowing. The next answer came to the question, "what do I do?" It was recommended to remove the tumor alone through a lumpectomy. But, every time I tried to make the appointment for the procedure I would have this intense fear overcome me, to the point of shaking.

Through this process, I became hyper aware of these signs. These are the signs that a scout uses when tracking something or someone. Signs like broken twigs, scat, and/or footprints are the signs of trackers. Daydreams, night dreams and body awareness's became the tracks I followed. Intuitive answers can come in many forms. Dreams are just a way messages can fly under the ego's radar.

Sometimes messages come through other people. The last time I had an intensive vision quest was after my divorce; I knew I needed to go back to school. Before this, I had attended non-accredited schools and apprenticed for my education in macrobiotic, and holistic studies. For three days I prayed, meditated and fasted by drinking tea and eating brown rice. I begged more than I prayed.

What do I do? Where do you want me? How can I serve? I spun the dynamo to generate answers.

I had taught macrobiotic, nutrition, and natural living for many years. I had studied with a healer and was two years into sobriety working with others in recovery. I focused on degrees in nutrition, counseling and education as the logical choice. Over the next three days of my "vision quest," three different people came to me and said,

"Be a nurse, be a nurse, and oh, by the way, be a nurse."

A novel thought, and in hindsight, was the best choice as I could teach, counsel and heal melding my holistic experience with allopathic approaches. Everything fell into place quickly, and I started nursing school shortly after accepting the guidance.

Everyone said I needed a lumpectomy, which would leave the breast intact and only remove the tumor. But I kept having panic attacks along with a repetitive vision of a gun going off into my breast and chest spreading cancer. I couldn't even schedule the appointment. Time and the tumor were not stopping their march. Though I wanted to keep my breast I could not ignore this intuitive sign the size of a boulder. I had to trust. I had asked, and I had gotten one answer.

My sober sponsor was one of many messengers who helped nudge me along. After the diagnosis, when I knew I would have to fight, but before I knew how, I was just doing the dietary change, still not sure what to do. I remember one conversation, my sponsor became very upset and started to yell,

> "I will not watch another person close to me commit suicide by not doing treatment!"

She had a friend who refused chemo and surgery and wanted to cure herself "naturally" and died. I heard her. I did take this as another, big sign. There were prior life experiences over the years that affirmed, I needed more than diet to control this now.

I did know, as a macrobiotic teacher, and holistic healer, many who had reversed cancer through natural approaches including diet. But the majority had some form of standard treatment along with natural foods and remedies. Though there were some rare people, who used strictly dietary treatments without conventional approaches, they were the exception. I had previous dreams and signs but did not act until I received my grandmom's message. Waiting as long as I did and having the type of cancer preempted strictly natural approaches. So the signs confirmed.

Also, I knew some who had their cancer reversed through standard medical treatments, which did well initially but never made any lifestyle, or dietary, changes. Their cancers come back, or never they fully recovered from the effects of the treatments to regain health and vitality.

It was twilight. I stood on the darkening lawn of my childhood home. There was a massive, roiling tent of caterpillars swarming up to my waist height. From the right, someone shoved a gasoline hose into the swarming mass. In a blink the mass was flat and the caterpillars were gone. Another dream. Apparently, I needed to find gas but not for my car.

The oncologist I called was from the closest cancer center.

"Yes, we do neo-adjuvant chemotherapy.

Giving chemo first (neo-adjuvant) before surgery was once a common practice, especially when tumors were found late and large.

"We can start you tomorrow.

The lady taking my information over the phone said,

"Oh this will be easy, you are already in the system."

Apparently, I had seen this doctor several years prior for pernicious anemia. I had forgotten that. The stars were aligning. I began chemo the next day. With just one treatment the tumor decreased by half in size and the pain ceased.

Nearing the end of my treatment, I had another vision. Seeing myself from several feet away, I was flat chested. Both my breast were gone. Though this was another clear guidance, I did not have the strength of an Amazon, the ancient Greek women warriors who lopped off breasts to improve their archery in battle.

> I remember talking to God, "Well if you want me to take them off I want a decent reconstruction. Please don't let me wake up without breasts."

Oh to be so demanding. My God didn't mind, after all, it was my choice. But there would be consequences.

I had a skin-sparing mastectomy on the affected side, a seven-hour surgery that went for 10 hours followed by complications. Skin-sparing meant the inner part of the breast was removed, the outer skin of my breast was saved. I woke up with a beautiful looking reconstructed breast but had to sacrifice my latissimus muscle, the largest muscle in the back. The plan was to do the other breast as a preventive measure. Certainly, This was not the flat chest of my vision.

I had two more cancer recurrences in the same breast close to where the tumor had been. After having cancer the third time, I had the reconstructed breast removed. With great relief, I finally removed my other breast as a preventive measure in 2014. The original vision finally fulfilled. I continue on anti-hormonal medication and feeling better every day despite multiple surgeries, treatments, and too many complications to detail. Recently, I have "seen" my chest with small breasts. I will venture to explore new options once done my current master's program I have much more peace and acceptance of my body and me, so the urgency to correct has lifted.

Foresight verses hindsight, no matter how clear the pre-vision, hindsight is always clearer. If I had followed the original vision of the bilateral mastectomy could I have avoided all of the problems? Maybe, I would not have gone through the recurrences. I certainly wouldn't have the chronic pain from complications of losing the latissimus muscle from my back. Through much processing I have been able to forgive myself for the choices I made. Self-forgiveness, though not easy, is a requirement to get relief from the slave master of regret.

So, what does a cancer journey have to do with entrepreneurship? When facing this challenge, I began to come to terms only when I saw it as my job. This business that required full time plus to manifest and manage. Each episode of cancer required a full year focus and multiple years of recovery. What more did I have to do but succeed at this one goal to overcome cancer and heal?

Financially, this was not a lucrative business, and I eventually went on disability, which though not anywhere near a windfall, helped pay for insurances and some basics. I was able to work part-time as a home care nurse until it was time to move on to pursue my gifts and further my education.

I was intuitively guided to go back to school again. I got my Bachelors in Nursing while completing chemotherapy for the third time. Currently, I am in a Masters program to become a psychiatric mental health nurse practitioner. Intuition has guided me the whole way. Except for at times, my ego was running rampant. I ignored insight and sometimes saw the results immediately and sometimes years later. Many times the results seemed negative but had a protective aspect not understood until years later.

There are much more tales to tell of honing intuition and rejecting it. "You didn't just direct me into psychiatry, God?" One of many arguments with God ended in acceptance then, understanding. Yes, asking means getting responses that seem outright contrary to everything logic dictates. But arguments are like looking at longed for gift horses in the mouth.

Premonitions and intuition were part of daily life growing up.

My mother would say aloud, "I wonder how your aunt Mary is?"

Within the next breath, the phone would ring, and my mom's sister would be on the phone. Early, I also had premonitions, visions, and the occasional vivid dream that was premonitory. In my teens, I had several dreams that predicted the pregnancies of some acquaintances that did not know they were pregnant at the time.

In the mid 70's I volunteered with disabled children at a state hospital. One of the staff workers who was a close friend of a cousin had difficulty getting pregnant which cause her heartache.

So, when I had a dream of her, I called her right away. She told me that she didn't think she was pregnant so I let it go.

When she had her first child eight months later, I visited her and the new baby.

"Remember that dream I had that you were pregnant?
She responded, "No, remind me what was it again?
"You were in this long, fitted, black polyester dress slowly walking up this steep hill in the wilderness."
She looked at me strangely and said, "That's weird, I wore a black dress just like that to the hospital when I went into labor."

I had not told her the details of the dream before this, just that I had a dream of her pregnant.

Over the years there were times in my life that this ability was more vivid than others. One of my teachers, Michio Kushi, talked of seeing the ancestors and the spirits, of dead relatives of the attendees of a conference.

He said, "When you look around at everyone here, you only see the physical people. What I see is a room full of you and all of your ancestors, and the spirits of those connected with each of you."

Michio's *The Book of Do-In* had exercises for honing the ability to see auras, spirits and ancestors that I began practicing, I had been eating very cleanly, almost to the point of fasting, was meditating, praying, and chanting the Heart Sutra. I began to see and hear spirits of people who had passed, and I freaked out. I was around 23 years old and felt way out of my depth. I broadened my diet and stopped the intensive practices. I needed to insulate the lightning rod, my antennae, and sixth sense.

Though I had improved and maintained my intuitive feelings, I did not see spirits so vividly after this. The mediumship subsided, and I was happy about it. My intuition was more internal and came through the dreams, visions, and feelings I was comfortable. I could deal with this. It wasn't until many years later that I would allow myself see the subtle realms to this degree.

Intuition takes many forms, and we all have it. It is a gut feeling, a hunch, a knowing without knowing, or logic.

> Steve Jobs said, "Have the courage to follow your heart and intuition. They somehow know what you truly want to become."

Experience has shown that some people use this without even knowing they have it. Others have keen abilities naturally or have worked hard to develop intuition. Just like some are born very athletic and physically inclined, others are born with sensitivities and skills considered supernatural. Some people come into strong intuitive abilities after trauma either physical and/or psychological.

The "mundane" of daily life becomes magical when we see the world intuitively. Seeing intuitively is seeing with the heart. There is the feeling of energies and the subtle nature of people and circumstances that are perceived. Many relate intuition as a gut feeling. For me, it has gone from gut to my heart. I see my part of the experience as a small piece of a puzzle that uniquely fits into the greater scheme of things.

Intuition, for me, is as natural and as necessary as breathing. Intuition is seeing the world with an expanded heart. Intuition is natural and a tool to live by. Living with this grace gives hope in the darkest of times. Though intuition we may not be able to avoid all of the difficulties of life the grace of intuition can help find meaning and peace no matter where the journey of life leads.

Nola E. Masterson

I have been blessed. I was the first analyst on Wall Street for biotechnology, at the same time that I started a consulting business which allowed me to work with the best venture capital firm in San Francisco and learn the art of creating new businesses. I have worked with the captains of the biotech industry and started a DNA analysis business which went public in 2000 and provided me with more money in founder stock than I had ever dreamed of having. I became a venture capitalist with a European venture firm and now I am a university professor, giving guidance to young startup companies and sitting on the Boards of exciting new technology private and public companies.

Moving Mountains With Love

Nola E. Masterson

In 1983 I sat in my new rental home, boxes still unpacked, staring at the street and wondering what I was going to do. I was soon to be a twice divorced, single mother of a two year old, and getting a lawyer to fight the company I had worked with for 8 years to obtain a decent severance package. I needed time, and I needed a cushion of money, health care and a car to create my new life. I was sad, angry and excited by the freedom to create my life anew.

How did a nice Catholic girl get herself into such a mess? My mother had told me as a young girl I had to be nicer than other girls because I was prettier, so I tried.

My baby was beautiful and I loved her so much. I had wanted to be a mother all my life, especially after being the second born and first girl in a family of six. I had tried to heal the wounds of the past, two husbands in Vietnam, divorced parents, but now I had created a situation which had to be solved with "out of the box" thinking. I was scared and motivated at the same time.

I had been given the name of my new business creation "Science Futures" in a clear lightning bolt message from the Universe a year ago. Now I had to manifest what that name was to be. So I went to work. I set up day care for as little time as possible and worked late into the night, meeting with venture capitalists to secure consulting work in biotechnology, my field, but a new one. I had a science degree, a medical technology degree and I had nine years of sales experience selling diagnostic and scientific products and being a regional manager training others to tap into the power of sales. Now, I was the product.

What I knew about biotechnology was new to the world and not many people had the vision of what was coming. A new age of biological-based products, from food and drugs to diagnostics and agriculture seeds. I knew it cold, and I could teach it, but to whom? I wanted to learn how money made money, so eventually I could stop working for money, but that was not taught in school. So I took a weekend course in becoming a consultant and decided to find clients in the finance world so I could learn about finance while I taught biotechnology.

I wanted to support this new entrepreneurial industry and I wanted to support my daughter. I was overwhelmed with the responsibility of being a single parent and breadwinner. I had to take charge, and that meant separate from my husband and my former company and start a new life. It was painful, sad and so very hurtful to my little girl. I didn't want her to see how sick her father was, and I didn't want her to think his behavior was her fault, as children have such an emotional view of the world, I knew she would not understand why he acted as he did. I wanted to spare her, and so I did what I thought best, after much prayer, counseling and the desire not to be a co-dependent.

I was lucky to meet a Wall Street analyst, who coached me and taught me how to write for Wall Street, as I educated the early fund managers about the new companies called Genentech, and Applied BioSystems. In my consulting to the venture capitalists in San Francisco who had created these new companies, I got my training and the early investors were eager to support and create the next new thing in biotechnology. I learned by consulting how to read business plans, and how to put together early teams to create the new pharmaceutical and device companies that would exploit the use of recombinant DNA and monoclonal antibodies.

These were areas of science that were changing the way drug discovery was done, and the business models for companies, that I had witnessed as a sales person to pharmaceutical companies, was changing, thanks to the pioneering efforts of California scientists and venture capitalists.

I had confidence and vision that what I had learned would be important to share with others. And I was learning from the best how to create new companies. One of the most empowering days was when Brook Byers, a pioneering biotech investor, said he wanted to know what I thought, in a meeting in front of other men. I wasn't just a pretty face, but a valued brain in a world of financiers. Teach what you know, to those whom you want learn from, that's the lesson I still give young people today.

That was where I found myself in the early 80's, and since then, I created a life based on that early inspiration of Science Futures. I have learned along the way to seek out mentors for every phase of my business career and also to find spiritual and physiological teachers who have helped me evolve. Many of the people who helped me didn't know they were also mentoring me. I learned from the nannies who helped me take care of the home and my little family. I learned from the choir members in my church, and from the clients and scientists I helped, many other women helped me. I studied human behavior and how to change your thinking from Christopher Howard. My most influential book was *The Power of Now* by Eckhart Tolle.

Because I was blazing new ways of working, not taking a job with a corporation, but setting up my own office, it was important to be self-directed. I did this by setting yearly goals which interested me, what science did I think was going to be important to learn? I would go to meetings and seminars which focused on that area of science or medicine, and strangely enough, that seemed to be the areas I was asked to consult on with others that year.

It was a career based on inspiration. I looked at the new industry that was being created like a mother looks at her growing child, what it would take to support it this year, and the next.

I did have two men who initially mentored and hired me to work, in venture and Wall Street, and helped me believe in myself and what I had to say. Brook Byers, a venture partner at Kleiner Perkins Caufield and Byers and Richard Vietor, a pharmaceutical analyst at Drexel Burnham Lambert both saw what I saw, that biotechnology was going to impact the world of business in a huge way. I will be forever grateful to them for teaching me the early skills of putting a new company together, and writing and communicating with investors.

For the next six years I had work to do which was exciting and profitable to me, and was able to feed my little family and provide support for a fledgling science-based industry. I was able, with their support, to grow into a leader and industry spokesperson for biotechnology. I wished, at that time, I could have gone to school for an MBA, but decided that getting one by doing would have to be my way. On the job training is as valuable as sitting in the classroom, if you are lucky enough to have good mentors.

I was comfortable working from home, as my years in sales and sales management with Bayer and Millipore had demanded that skill set. Now with the concurrent development of desktop computers, my type of consulting and advising was going to become a viable option for many people. My clients needed information that was current and so did I. I encouraged another young mother, and scientist, who was skilled in writing to begin a monthly newsletter, which we called BioVenture View. I was able to provide sales of that publication to her, and she was launched as a mouthpiece for biotechnology. That job of an industry publication was done.

I saw a need to bring biotech leaders together, and had an idea for a conference which would be invitation only, including the spouses of CEOs, in 1985. Brook and I called that meeting:

"The Biotech Meeting in Laguna Nigel"

And the first meeting was a huge success, and still occurs today. That job of providing a networking conference was done.

I followed my Wall Street mentor to Merrill Lynch when he changed firms and we hired a full time analyst to work with him in New York, to cover biotech stocks. I continued to consult, but my example of following biotechnology stocks was being picked up by others, so I felt that the job of coverage on Wall Street for venture backed stocks was being done, and I could start to focus on writing business plans. The opportunity to do that came from Brook, as he asked me to write the first plan for Idec Pharmaceuticals, an idea which came from his San Diego friend Ivor Royston MD. Ivor and Brook had done two previous deals, Hybritech and GenProbe.

When GenProbe was ready to go public, in late 1987, I lobbied for Merrill Lynch to be the bankers, by calling and asking all of the members of the board for the business. They agreed and I had my very first "tombstone". Being a woman was still a novel role in venture and on Wall Street. At the post IPO party I was given as a gag, the wet tee shirt award. These slights and sexist remarks to today's generation of woman may offend, but to me, it was just the way of MAD MEN, and I had seen it before in my career in sales. I felt that, any woman who came after me would be judged by my example, and that was a weight I consciously carried.

I had developed a long term plan because I was acting as both mother and father, my ultimate goal was to become a venture capitalist and sit on boards of directors. I wasn't sure how I was going to do that, but I set my intention. I worked with clients I could learn from and evolved the plan. After all, I did have a master's degree from George Washington University and I knew biotech science because of my 8 years in sales to the scientists who were inside the early biotech companies. I was confident that I could see a future which would allow me to have a work/life balance that included being a mother and a success in business.

I was fully present and I listened to others with an open mind and articulating heart based on my philosophy of win-win. If I took on a client I had to be sure I could provide a valuable end product or service. Confidence was key and I was the message. My years of training others in sales came in handy as I was able to have stage presence and presentation skills. I had a personal and professional cause which excited me. Yet, I could not ignore my spirit, which was just as important as the intellectual part of my life.

I value love, used it as a guiding principal in my life, and found it in relationships with friends and family. My daughter was my deepest love, and she was growing rapidly. After 8 years of giving my all to my biotechnology consulting practice, and working with clients I felt the courage to try again at marriage.

Through a blind date, I met my husband, a lawyer who enjoyed working with startup companies, and was also a single father although his daughter lived with her mother. The girls were 5 years apart in age. Neither of us wanted to play the dating game anymore and so we all took vows six months later and agreed to "try and cooperate" as a family, knowing full well that there would be ups and downs.

It was refreshing to be more realistic and not base the relationship on fantasy that someday my soul mate would come. We are earth walk partners, and we support each other's walk on earth at this time.

I lost my mother 3 months after the wedding, and 4 months later my daughter's father died, and we buried him with a 21 gun salute in the Presidio cemetery. Such a loss to both my daughter and me, but there was more to come, as our dog of 11 years died, and then my Dad.

It was all I could do to function, let alone be a mom and a new bride. My husband kept a safe distance while I grieved and I was led to find new ways to heal, with a grief therapist for my mind and network chiropractic care for my body. I learned Jin Shin Do acupressure, taking classes for 18 months as a way to explore a more Eastern style of medicine, which was profoundly healing. The meridian system of the body was as interesting to me as DNA and 5,000 years of study by the Asian cultures gave me a perspective on the healing arts which incorporated my earlier study of the I Ching and the universal Chi energy.

Shortly after my father's death I had a breakthrough, in which I realized that I had allies on the "other side" who would guide and direct my career if I let them. I decided to take a big risk by starting my own biotechnology company with a German co-founder, Hubert Koster. He had the idea to get the mass weight of DNA, and a genetic analysis company was born, named Sequenom. We worked together for 7 years, I was the founding CEO and a member of the Board, and the company went public in 2000. Initially to launch the company I started another industry conference, this time in Europe, to connect the large pharmaceutical companies with the smaller startup ventures in the USA. I modeled it after the Laguna Nigel event and held the first meeting in Cannes, France. I met at this first conference a venture capitalist from TVM Capital, Germany's largest venture fund, Helmut Schuehsler, and introduced him to Hubert and suggested that he would be wise to invest in Sequenom, which had German roots. He did, and our relationship became very supportive for the next 14 years. I was impressed with the culture of the European venture firms as they were extremely intelligent and very polite. TVM launched many good new companies, but Sequenom was one of their biggest successes.

I learned a lot from the experience of launching Sequenom, from asking for more stock every time I did something noteworthy for the company, to replacing myself as CEO and on the Board when it was appropriate. Knowing how to step off is as important as stepping on to a role. It is called power jumping, or orchestrating transitions. Hubert was brilliant, a genius, and yet it took 4 years after the birth of the company to give him the title of CEO, because he was so professorial in his mannerism and style.

At the last round of financing before the public offering I was negotiating with a Swiss venture capitalist and I could tell he was uncomfortable with a woman on the Board. I promised him that if he made a large investment I would replace myself with a very qualified man, which I did. This proved to be a gift to me, because when the company went public I was free to sell my founders shares unlike other employees who were locked up and could not cash out on the stellar IPO performance.

I started my own venture fund in the late 90's to practice the skill sets needed to understand the back office of venture capital. This first fund was used to invest in TVM's first all medical venture fund and would allow my investors to participate in the fourth round of venture capital in Sequenom and also to invest in a German Deutsche Mark fund which would return profits in Euros. This first fund of funds was followed by another small fund which invested some of the profits from my shares in Sequenom. I wanted to go bigger, so I created the necessary documents, for Tahoe Venture Partners, and obtained a partner, and set out to get investors. In the process Helmut offered me a proposal I couldn't refuse. Rather than start my own fund, he proposed that I join TVM and open their San Francisco office and help raise the TVM fifth fund. They were the largest venture fund in Germany and I was now part of their team.

Then, the unexpected happened: the events of 9/11 in 2001. This caused TVM to backtrack from its goals in the U.S. as the country suddenly became a very unfriendly place for Europeans in terms of flying and security. TVM made the decision to only have an East Coast office and so two and a half years after opening the San Francisco office it was closed. While this changed my course with the company, I was kept on as an advisor for five years, getting me closer to my ultimate goal. This unexpected transition expanded my horizons.

I accepted a nomination to join the Board of Directors of ReprosTherapeutics Inc. in Houston. For the next five years I served on various committees including the Audit, Nominating, and the Compensation committees. In November, of 2009 the company announced that I was appointed Chair of the Board. This followed a shareholder activist battle in which I was able to support the CEO at a critical time in the company's development.

I was effectively transitioning into being a very good Board leader. One of my personal goals that I had set 25 years earlier was achieved.

Although my professional goals were being met, I still felt uneasy with the hurt and pain of the demise of my first two marriages as a result of both husbands' service in Vietnam. The post war trauma still haunted me and somehow I wanted to make myself right with that country. I was invited to join a fact finding mission with 15 highly successful women from the high tech industry to learn how Vietnam was running from a woman's point of view. This was the way I wanted to see Vietnam! The group took off in February 2008 and met with men and women in Hanoi and Ho Chi Minh City to assess Vietnam's economy, schools, thoughts regarding ex-patriots, and goals of the ministers of trade and finance. We were very excited about the growth and entrepreneurial spirit of the people we met and the lack of animosity towards Americans. After all, they had won the war, and we were a minor player in the century of their fighting with the French and the Chinese.

I left a lot of pain, fear and blood on my hands behind during that trip and became very excited about the Vietnamese publicly traded stock markets. I had learned how to trade in biotechnology stocks in the 1980's and now Vietnam had a ten year old public market which was just taking off.

The very young people in the banking houses were happy to explain to us how their market worked, and it seemed like the perfect spot to support the country. Given my experience in fund management I created a Vietnam investment fund consisting of a blue chip list of 15 Vietnamese publicly traded companies that allowed foreigners to buy in. The fund supported the country's infrastructure and participated in building a middle class in Vietnam. This was my way to heal my heart and help build the economy at the same time. I now think of Vietnam in an entirely different light and have several Vietnamese friends.

If I know that love is myself and that pain is also myself, that understanding is myself, that understanding is myself and suffering too, then I will be mindful. I will not suppress my own suffering because I know that I can transform it into a flower... The flower exists because the suffering exists.

— Thich Nhat Hanh, the Vietnamese monk

It was a profound healing for me to go to Vietnam and meet the people whom my husbands had called "the enemy". I gained a sense of peace by listening to their side of the war, and to realize how long I had carried the scars and how much the Vietnamese people had been able to move on. The young Vietnamese men and women called it their parents' war. The people my age said it was in the past and the present was all there is, with a look of sadness that I was still carrying the past in my present.

One woman I met, and had an intimate dinner with, had been a baby in the hospital in Hanoi. Her father took her out and got her home, an hour before we bombed that hospital. She went to college at Boston University to learn what kind of people bomb hospitals. She was teaching at the Economic University in Hanoi, and also had alcoholism in her marriage. I have an open invitation to come back and teach her students, in English. Sharing with other women helped heal my soul.

I went back to Vietnam on my own a year later, and met with a venture capitalist who surprisingly went to my high school in Virginia. I marvel at how connected we all are from a heart level. I traveled to China and found their culture to be honoring of my early work of creating IDEC and Sequenom. That country is in the midst of an entrepreneurial boom and they are anxious to learn. Travel expanded my sense of self in the world and gave me a sense of adventure, which I love.

I now teach a course at the University of San Francisco, entitled the Local, National and Global Biotech, and the students are the source of my learning. I mentor young CEOs and sit on Boards of public and private companies. As co-chair of the Women Corporate Directors Northern California Chapter, I am gaining a global perspective of women on boards across the globe. I can share with others the wisdom of my journey which is still unfolding. I continue to learn how to be a good Board member and coach, and wife and mother. Being able to have a sense of my own history allows me to support the success and failure in companies and navigate the twists and turns with others more joyfully now.

Be the creator of your own life. You are here for a reason. There is nothing accidental about you. That was the message of Science Futures. I figured out my specific purpose and found my mission on Earth. I found mentors and family to support my assignment and I realized my specialness.

It is our way of seeing the world that determines the nature of our feelings

—Thich Nhat Hanh

Janet Taylor

Janet Taylor is a mother, owner of a multi-million dollar insurance brokerage, life coach, writer and will also be launching her own line of holistic skin care. Her other interests are holistic medicine and helping others with their business aspiration.

Janet can be reached at
janet@reclaimingmysoul.com

Sanctuary of the Soul

Janet Taylor

My hope for you is that you will realize that you are special, blessed, gifted and have boundless potential. If you are feeling tired, used, trapped and lonely I am hoping to help you see things within yourself differently. Those who succeed through adversity are the ones who believe they will get to the other side, rely on themselves to get there, and NEVER feel like a victim to the circumstance that they're trying to get through.

If you find yourself feeling like you are stuck in quick sand in life, related to your finances, relationship, career or health, keep digging and don't look up. If you have gotten to the point where the quick sand is just about moved, dig longer and harder to make sure you have a lot of wiggle room because an earthquake might be just around the next corner. Never take a comfortable place for granted. Appreciate it! Be truly, humbly, grateful for it, but work really hard to maintain it because things can change quickly.

Growing up my life was easy in a stereotypical 60's family with loving parents, a mom who stayed home to care for us and a dad that worked hard to provide for us. Although we did not have a lot, my parents made us feel rich. Reflecting back, I realize how important all of that was for shaping me into an adult who is confident and comfortable with myself.

Going through life with love and respect for yourself as well as with the confidence to know you are ultimately in control of what happens to you and where your life leads is the foundation for a healthy mind and soul. I am grateful for being provided with this exact foundation and I know not everyone has been as lucky as I was.

As I entered adolescence and spent time with schoolmates I noticed that some of my peers were sad, mad, or wounded and lacked confidence. Some even found joy in hurting others to feel better about themselves. Now that I've had more years and experiences on this earth, I know that with coming from a nurturing and loving home is not always enough for some and others that come from a troubled home grow up into wonderful, whole and loving people. You are not a product of your circumstance whether good or bad. You are ultimately a product of yourself.

We live in a society of competitive arrogance, jealousy, entitlement, excuses and acceptance to a fault. What has become of us, other than a product of the wearing away of our true values and ultimately our true selves?

Life has become so difficult for many that it is a rarity to find someone who nourishes your soul instead of feeding from it with their emptiness, negativity and drama. It is a challenge to be truly happy inside when you are surrounded by so much gloominess and so many people that exhaust you. No matter what age or stage we are at in life all of us have preconceived images of what we would like our life to be moving forward. However, as we have all learned, life does not necessarily always line up with your imagination, expectations, or desires and preferences.

Life is very fluid and constantly changing. You only have control over yourself, your thoughts, your actions and nothing or no one else. Many of us endure tough issues and circumstances, like feeling left out, divorce, financial hardships, parenting that does not go the way we would like it to, friendships that we outgrow and family members that we find we can't rely on or who zap us of our energy. All of these things chip away at our suit of armor leaving us vulnerable to the next rescue when we barely have enough energy to get ourselves to shore to rest and rebalance ourselves.

If we ignore ourselves, our own needs, we eventually slip away from our center. To me our center is our soul which is wiser and older and knows us better than we do. It is our guiding light, home of our guardian angels and a place that is not prejudiced by our constant changes in life. It is always there, always solidly on our side and something that can never be taken away from us.

When you are raw enough to feel it, and connect with it, you will know what I mean by the inner energy you will feel and that which I am referring to. It is a place of rejuvenation, comfortable silence and truth. It is also the part of you that makes you question a decision. It is your true self.

Loving yourself is your suit of armor

As we all know we only have control over ourselves, our actions and how we treat others but also how we treat ourselves. When we realize that loving yourself is the suit of armor needed to fend off intruders to our emotional energy we can begin to heal from the exhaustive journey we might have found ourselves on.

There are many wonderful things about loving and respecting yourself. When people meet you they will be attracted to it and want to be around you to find out your secret. Unfortunately the wounded, empty and searching will seek you out like a moth towards a light. It is not easy for us to turn away.

We are full of inner strength and know we not only face every situation from a place of humble confidence we also have a low immune system when we see someone we care about suffering, and we go into rescue mode to share our energy with them. So often they become an energy drain and sometimes that can be like an emotional vampire.

Without them having their own inner love and confidence, no matter how much of your energy reserves and soul you share with them, it is only a temporary fix for them and they will be back for more. It becomes a constant struggle to keep your energy in balance when you are in relationships like this.

Sometimes the closest people to us are the ones that continue to do this to us. We realize what is happening but we cannot walk away. To cope we shut ourselves down little by little until we lose touch with our inner spring of energy and start to disconnect with our soul and truth as a defense mechanism.

As we shut ourselves down we become resentful, feel hurt, used, and weary and seek ways to make ourselves feel better - usually outside of ourselves.

If you were a strong swimmer and you saw someone drowning, you would certainly dive into the water to help. That person might latch onto you knowing you are their only hope. In doing so they could be so desperate that they pull you under the water in their struggle to survive. Do you continue to try and save them or swim away to save your own life knowing you might be lost to the water and somehow they will use your spiritless body to sustain themselves until another rescuer comes along?

Confidence is your light

Confidence in yourself is as important as your loving suit of armor. Envision it as your light that guides you along your path. This is also the light that others will see beaming from you and want to be around to bask and rejuvenate in. This light is born in your soul from its many gifts that are boundless when we stay connected to it.

Although it is important to listen to others' opinions objectively, with open ears and an open heart, ultimately the decision to be made is your own, for you, in that moment. You are the one that will have to live and thrive within the decisions you have made. At times you will most likely discover that your decision might not have been the best as time goes on but, there again, it is a lesson you will be grateful to have walked through when you thrive on the other side of it.

Your inner truth is your shield

Going through life being true to yourself and who you are is your shield. That truth is not for you to hide behind – it is for you to lead with to the places you are going to find yourself in during your journey. It is also your compass when you find yourself off track or being pulled into someone else's truth for you. Your shield is something important for you to get to know and be comfortable with when you are feeling weak to an energy drawer or someone that lives by the sword. Although some dents in your shield are destined to occur, it is important to love and accept those dents as badges of what you have battled through. Lovingly cherishing and caring for your truth is constant work but so vital to protecting, loving and respecting every part of you.

Trusting in yourself are your wings

Trusting in yourself are your wings. It allows you to soar, take on new challenges, and never be victim to anyone's negative feedback telling you that you are going to fail. Even more importantly never listening to the mortal chatter inside of your own head that is based in fear, insecurity, and is not from a loving, and supporting place of truth in your soul. At times you will find your soul, heart and mind all pulling you in different directions and working independently of each other. The inner wisdom of your soul always knows best. With this trust anything is possible in the end.

You often might need to make many attempts to take flight and stay on course, but the skills within you can re-evaluate, rejuvenate, and tweak your flight plan. Sometimes the destination you originally set out for changes along the way because of a storm you found yourself in or one you were trying to avoid. This is most likely part of the master plan no matter how frustrating or deflating it is. Be diligent; that obstacle might be heading you in a different but right direction without you even knowing it at the time. Be thankful and trust yourself through it. Never lose trust in yourself and your capabilities.

Loving others is your strength

When you consciously connect to your soul and feel the abundant positive loving energy running through you cannot help but see life differently. This becomes your strength built from love. A sunset looks more beautiful and stirs within you a deeper feeling of awe. You feel the grass below your feet as a living carpet set out to soften your steps. Honesty and love within yourself allows you to look into people's eyes and connect with them on a deeper level even if your time with them is a brief encounter. They will feel your love and hopefully you will feel theirs restoring your energy like a cold drink on a hot day. Although encounters like this for many of us within our busy days are rare, I think if you practice them, you will find them more often by creating them. People respond to positive feelings because we are all searching for those feelings in many different ways.

Retreating when necessary is your soft place to land

As vital as everything I have asked you to find within yourself is the importance of retreating to a place that allows you time to heal, rest, restore, feel inspired and it is crucial to the essentials of everything else. Although this place is always within you, having a physical place to go and withdraw helps embody it. These places can be created from anywhere you find yourself during your daily journey. For some it might be a corner of the couch, a favorite chair, a space in your yard, a place in your office where you can shut the world off for as much time as you need, or have, to be still, quiet and re-center yourself. Some are able to get this through meditation, which is not easy for everyone, including myself. You can get similar feelings by consciously being quiet, quieting your mind and traveling within concentrating on you, your breathing, the way you are feeling. Just relax and drink from that inner fountain of loving, healing energy within you. Give yourself that vital time out. Without it your emotional (and physical) immune system becomes compromised to drama, negativity and stress which will start the process of detachment from within.

My adult life has been full of challenges, adversity, hard decisions, life changing health issues and many ups and downs. Through each one of them I knew I had the tools to make it through whatever curve ball came my way. That knowledge came from within me, from my soul. Every one of those hard times has led me here and made me who I am. No one can take away what I have experienced, learned, and survived - it is mine to be grateful for and they are the roots of my existence. I am a constant work in progress and I look forward to learning from each blessing and challenge that comes my way.

As I sit here in a house I have lived in for 17 years in which there have been so many life changes I am about to embark on yet another. A lot of my life changes were challenges of every kind that I had to see not only myself through but also my two daughters - who became the wind beneath my wings and my driving force to be strong and persevere. I am more grateful than anything else in my life that we were teamed up to go through this life together.

Now they are grown, living on their own, and starting their own families. Together we had so many cold nights in this house wearing extra layers and having extra blankets on the bed to make the heating oil last as long as we could. Sometimes that did not go as planned, and so now I can even prime an oil burner after getting diesel from the gas station to get the heat going.

Their having a mother who was trying to get a business off the ground so I could keep us in this house and having to take them with me to work most days was not easy for them.

Our biggest challenge was when they were 9 and 11 and I had a medical emergency that left me with a brain injury. There was no time to spend asking why or to wonder how I was going to be able to keep us all going. The only solution was to keep moving forward every day. My occupational therapy was going to work.

To string words together while speaking with clients or in written communication was beyond exhausting. Trying to figure how to use the simple office equipment I had used every day prior became a frustrating challenge.

Even though the kids were very young we worked together like a school of fish. They instinctively knew what to do without me asking. When I had trouble stringing together those words to make a sentence while talking they would smoothly interject the correct word to keep my sentence flowing. When my equilibrium was so off that I would drive too close to the right side of the road they became my back seat drivers alerting me (by screaming) that I almost hit a telephone pole or mailbox that we just passed. Those trips were made on angel's wings and I swear the right mirror of my car passed miraculously through so many telephone poles during that time. We made it through not only surviving but actually thriving as a team!

So many years ago when I was being discouraged to start my own business and heard a lot of "I told you so's" along the way, I never doubted myself even though I seemingly had every odd stacked against me. I did not have a college degree, or money, I had a two year old and my second daughter was just a few months away from being born.

There were so many tough times but through them I discovered the hidden gems within myself that we all have. My love and respect for myself, the self-assurance that I could be successful, my inner truth to protect me and guide me, my confidence to help me soar and the tremendous love and dedication to my two daughters. Also making sure I always found a way to escape those busy, scary, chaotic times to quiet my mind, connect with my soul for guidance, wisdom and healing.

Today I finally feel like I have arrived at the top of a mountain I have been climbing for so many years, through so many storms and mudslides.

My life is about to change again. I have decided to move from this house as I have found beautiful land about an hour from the place that has for so long been home, in an area I had never been to before but felt guided to explore and I fell in love with! Many hours and months I spent physically walking on this parcel and going within for guidance.

It was also important for me to know that this slice of earthly heaven was accepting of me. When I was sure both were in balance, I went through many more months of sticky negotiation and finally made the purchase. I put my house on the market, which sold in a matter of hours in a bidding war. I feel so blessed, thankful and fortunate. Everything is aligning the way it is supposed to for my new path. I will only be in my current house for another two weeks and so I need to begin the daunting task of packing up. It is amazing how much stuff you collect throughout the years. As soon as I write the last line of this I will begin that task which will be bitter sweet.

Moving away from what is comfortable has finally become easy for me. Since the house went on the market I admit that I have had moments of 'seller's remorse' and wondering what the hell am I doing! But, with that said, I do feel an undercurrent and driving force that is encouraging me to move on and a confidence that I am standing on the edge of so many great things.

In order to afford the house that I want to build I have decided to General Contract the build myself. This is something I have never done. I have heard much doubt about me being able to achieve my dream. I am already starting to plan and prepare a guest list to my 'doubter's party' which I hope to have earlier than expected. I have faced so many challenges that might seem impossible to many but seems very possible to me. Understanding that sometimes things won't go as planned along the way is what keeps me sane and focused.

Our journey through life always continues and it is up to us to stay on the path that feels right for us and to deeply feel and be grateful for all of the wonderful experiences along the way. Know that there will also be some trying experiences along the way, but you need to be just as grateful for them as they are purposeful and make us who we are. Keep walking, with one foot in front of the other, change course when you need to, dig out when you find yourself in quick sand, don't allow yourself to be pulled under water by someone looking to be rescued, and don't let an emotional vampire sink their teeth into you. Always stay true to yourself with an open mind and heart to others along the way. Have the strength to withdraw from those that deplete you and take time to drink from your own soul. Use every grain of sand you have moved out of your way to make a string of pearls and wear them with pride.

You have every ingredient necessary
to succeed, thrive and be happy!
Remember the tools you were born with:
Loving yourself is your suit of armor
Confidence is your light
Inner truth is your shield
Trust in yourself are your wings
Loving others is your strength
Retreating and reconnecting with your
soul is your healing place.

Milton Keynes UK
Ingram Content Group UK Ltd.
UKHW021604110124
435868UK00010B/851

9 780692 076439